A SAMPLING OF INSPIRATION FROM
HAVE A GREAT DAY

April 10:
"The more I see of people the more I'm impressed by their astounding ability to meet tough situations. And their ability to rebound is fantastic. There is a built-in comeback power to you that should never be underestimated."

July 5:
"A positive thinker does not refuse to recognize the negative; he refuses to dwell on it. Positive thinking is a form of thought which habitually looks for the best results from the worst conditions."

November 11:
"An important question for anyone is: What am I doing to my own self? Am I making myself big to equate with the power potential in me? Or am I accepting smallness as all I am capable of? To think yourself smaller than you are is a violation of your real nature. Think big."

HAVE A GREAT DAY

Norman Vincent Peale

FAWCETT CREST • NEW YORK

Scripture quotations are from the King James Version of the Bible.

Excerpt from "The Spell of the Yukon" reprinted by permission of Dodd, Mead and Company, Inc., from THE COLLECTED POEMS OF ROBERT SERVICE.

A Fawcett Crest Book
Published by Ballantine Books
Copyright © 1985 by Norman Vincent Peale

Library of Congress Catalog Card Number: 84-13345

ISBN 0-449-20917-2

This edition published by arrangement with Fleming H. Revell Company and The K. S. Giniger Company, Inc.

Manufactured in the United States of America

First Ballantine Books Edition: October 1986

19 18 17 16 15 14 13 12 11 10

Contents

*With appreciation to
Nancy Dakin
for her help
in preparing
this
manuscript*

How to Use This Book

All of us, it seems, need something every day to keep us going with full energy and enthusiasm. And perhaps nothing is more effective than a motivating and inspiring thought.

There is an old saying, "An apple a day keeps the doctor away." May it not also be said that an upbeat thought a day will keep the shadows away and let in the bright light of hope and joy?

For many years, I have made it a practice to insert in my mind every day some inspiring thought and visualize it as seeping into my consciousness. My personal experience has been that such thoughts gradually permeate and affect attitudes. Sometimes I have called them "spirit lifters" for they do just that. And spirit lifting is needed by all of us.

At other times, I have called these selected ideas "thought conditioners." Even as the atmosphere of a room can be changed by air conditioning, so the climate of the mind can be changed by "thought conditioning." And a thought can make an enormous difference in how one feels mentally, emotionally, and physically. Certainly, to have a great day every day it helps to think great thoughts and to concentrate on at least one every day.

So, this book presents 366 upbeat and positive thoughts, one for every day in the year, including leap year. It is my hope that you will keep the book readily available on your desk, nightstand, in the kitchen, or perhaps have a copy in each place. If you begin to feel "down," take up the book and read the thought for the day. And if one isn't enough, read a few more of them.

Do not hesitate to mark thoughts that may especially appeal to you; turn down the pages and go back and read them again and again. Rereading helps to sink any helpful thought ever deeper into the mind. And the deeper a thought penetrates, the more powerful will be its effect upon your well-being.

Further, if you want to clip a thought out of the book to carry it in your wallet or pocket or handbag, don't let the notion that a book should not be mutilated stop you. A book is only a tool to be used for one's own good. And if you find you have hacked it up too much, you can always get another copy. The idea is that this book is a kind of medicine chest for healthy thinking. So, take the medicine and become a healthier, happier person.

Let me also suggest what I call the "shirt pocket technique." My shirt pocket is very important to me, for into it I put sayings and quotations written on cards. And, on some cards, I write my goals. Putting the cards into the pocket means placing the quotations over the heart, thus emphasizing the emotional factor. I read these cards repeatedly until, by a process of intellectual osmosis, they pass from the conscious to the subconscious mind and so become determinative.

But, however you use the daily thoughts in this day-by-day book, I truly hope they will help you to have a great day every day.

Norman Vincent Peale

JANUARY

January 1 --------------------------------------

At the New Year, we usually resolve to quit something. There is a psychological law of quitting. It's this: The more you keep quitting, the easier quitting becomes. I know, for I've spent a lot of time quitting fattening foods. But I finally discovered how to quit successfully. Quit for one meal, then two, then three. By now it begins to get tough. So you get tougher, quit the next day and the next. After a while, pride enters the picture to help you. You begin to boast about all the things you haven't eaten. Then you point with pride to your belt, for you have tightened it to the last notch. This is called positive quitting and can be applied to anything you want to change in your life.

January 2 --------------------------------------

Anybody can do just about anything with himself that he really wants to and makes up his mind to do. We all are capable of greater things than we realize. How much one actually achieves depends largely on: 1. Desire. 2. Faith. 3. Persistent effort. 4. Ability. But if you are lacking in the first three factors, your ability will not balance out the lack. So concentrate on the first three and the results will amaze you.

January 3 --

The way to success: First have a clear goal, not a fuzzy one. Sharpen this goal until it becomes specific and clearly defined in your conscious mind. Hold it there until, by the process of spiritual and intellectual osmosis of which I wrote in my introduction to this book, it seeps into your unconscious. Then you will have it because it has you. Surround this goal constantly with positive thoughts and faith. Give it positive follow-through. That is the way success is achieved.

January 4 --

To affirm a great day is a pretty sure way to have one. When awakening, get out of bed and stretch to your full height, saying aloud, "This is going to be a great day." What you say strongly is a kind of command, a positive, affirmative attitude that tends to draw good results to you.

January 5 --

Go forward confidently, energetically attacking problems, expecting favorable outcomes. When obstacles or difficulties arise, the positive thinker takes them as creative opportunities. He welcomes the challenge of a tough problem and looks for ways to turn it to advantage. This attitude is a key factor in impressive careers and great living.

January 6

At Dunkirk, the fate of the British nation hung upon getting the fighting men off the beaches and back to England. During the most difficult hour, a colonel rushed up to general Alexander, crying, "Our position is catastrophic!" The general replied: "Colonel, I don't understand big words. Just get busy and get those men out of here!" That's the kind of thinking needed in crises. Do the simple necessary.

January 7

Fear can infect us early in life until eventually it cuts a deep groove of apprehension in all our thinking. To counteract it, let faith, hope, and courage enter your thinking. Fear is strong, but faith is stronger yet. The Bible tells us, ". . . And he laid his right hand upon me, saying unto me, Fear not . . ." (Revelation 1:17). His hand is always upon you, too.

January 8

As an emotion, anger is always hot. To reduce an emotion, cool it. Some people count to ten, but perhaps the first ten words of the Lord's Prayer will work even better: "Our Father which art in heaven, Hallowed be thy name" (Matthew 6:9). Say that ten times and anger will lose its power.

January 9

Once, when I felt I had done an especially poor job in the pulpit on a Sunday morning, forgetting the best things I had to say and saying the poorest things, I was pretty discouraged. An old preacher, a polished orator in his day, patted me on the back. "Don't let it bother you, son," he said consolingly. "Forget it. The congregation will, and you might as well make it unanimous."

January 10

I shall never forget Ralph Rockwell. He was the farmer on our place in the country. Ralph was a New Englander of the old school, always caring for the place as though it were his own. He said to me once, when I was presuming to give him advice: "Tell you what, Dr. Peale, you do the preaching. I'll do the farming." It is good to remember to take advice as well as give it.

January 11

George Reeves was a huge man, 6 feet 2, weighing 240 pounds. He was my teacher in the fifth grade. In class, he would suddenly shout, "Silence." Then he would print in big letters on the blackboard the word CAN'T. Turning to the class, he would demand, "And now what shall I do?" Knowing what he wanted, we chanted back, "Knock the T off the CAN'T." With a sweeping gesture, he would erase it, leaving the word CAN. Dusting the chalk from his fingers, he would say, "Let that be a lesson to you—you *can* if you think you can."

January 12

The place was Korea, the hour midnight. It was bitter cold, the temperature below zero. A big battle was building for the morning. A burly U.S. marine was leaning against a tank eating cold beans out of a can with a penknife. A newspaper correspondent watching him was moved to propound a philosophical question: "Look," he said, "if I were God and could give you what you wanted most, what would you ask for?" The marine dug out another penknife of beans, thought reflectively, then said, "I would ask for tomorrow." Perhaps so would we all—a great tomorrow.

January 13 ━━━━━━━━━━━━━━━━━━━━━━━

My college classmate Judson Sayre started with nothing and became one of the most successful salesmen in our country. At dinner, in his apartment on Lake Shore Drive in Chicago, we got to talking about having a great day— for he was expert at it. "Come look at my mirror," he said. He had pasted a sign there which read:

> *Want a great day?*
> *Believe a great day.*
> *Pray a great day.*
> *Deserve a great day.*
> *Take God with you for a great day.*
> *Get going and make it a great day.*

January 14 ━━━━━━━━━━━━━━━━━━━━━━━

At one time I lived in upstate New York, where the winters are quite cold. And the roads would freeze and melt and freeze again. Come springtime, they were pretty badly broken up and rutted. One early April day, I came to a bad stretch of road where someone had put up a hand-made sign: "Choose your rut well. You'll be in it for the next twenty-five miles." Pretty good idea to get into the right rut, isn't it?

January 15 ————————————————————

Obviously, he was a happy man. He was Joe of Joe's Place, a little lunch counter I found one night. There were about a dozen stools occupied, for the most part by elderly men and a couple of older women from the neighborhood. He set a steaming bowl of soup before an old man whose hands shook. "Mamie made it special for you, Mr. Jones." One elderly and rather stumbling lady started to go out the door. "Be careful, Mrs. Hudson, the cars go pretty fast out there. And, oh yes, look at the full moon over the river. It's mighty pretty tonight." I sat there thinking that Joe was happy because he really loves people.

January 16 ————————————————————

The "as if" principle works. Act "as if" you were not afraid and you will become courageous, "as if" you could and you'll find that you can. Act "as if" you like a person and you'll find a friendship.

January 17 ————————————————————

Attitudes are more important than facts. Certainly, you can't ignore a fact, but the attitude with which you approach it is all-important. The secret of life isn't what happens to you but what you do with what happens to you.

January 18

You can do amazing things if you have strong faith, deep desire, and just hang in there.

January 19

The best of all ways to get your mind off your own troubles is to try to help someone else with theirs. As an old Chinese proverb says, "When I dig another out of trouble, the hole from which I lift him is the place where I bury my own."

January 20

Said William James, "Believe that you possess significant reserves of health, energy, and endurance, and your belief will help create the fact."

January 21

A man who had suffered a succession of devastating blows said something I liked: "I came through because I discovered a comeback quality had been built into me."

January 22

A whimsical old preacher, speaking on a familiar text, said, "And now abideth faith, hope, and love, these three, but the greatest of these is common sense."

January 23

Don't knock yourself out trying to compete with others. Build yourself up by competing with yourself. Always keep on surpassing yourself.

January 24

Work and live *enthusiastically*. Take successes *gratefully*. Face failures *phlegmatically*—that is, with a "so what?" attitude. And aim to take life as it comes, philosophically.

January 25

Yesterday ended last night. Every day is a new beginning. Learn the skill of forgetting. And move on.

January 26

Self-confidence and courage hinge on the kind of thoughts you think. Nurture negative thoughts over a long period of time and you are going to get negative results. Your subconscious is very accommodating. It will send up to you exactly what you send down to it. Keep on sending it fear and self-inadequacy thoughts and that is what it will feed back to you. Take charge of your mind and begin to fill it with healthy, positive, and courageous thoughts.

January 27

There is a three-point program for doing something with yourself. Find yourself, motivate yourself, commit yourself. These three will produce results.

January 28

The famous Olympic champion Jesse Owens said that four words made him: *Determination. Dedication. Discipline. Attitude.*

January 29

Do not exclusively say your prayers in the form of asking God for something. The prayer of thanksgiving is much more powerful. Name all the fine things you possess, all the wonderful things that have happened to you, and thank God for them. Make that your prayer.

January 30

The controlled person is a powerful person. He who always keeps his head will always get ahead. Edwin Markham said, "At the heart of the cyclone tearing the sky is a place of central calm." The cyclone derives its powers from a calm center. So does a person.

January 31

Theodore Roosevelt, a strong and tough-minded man, said: "I have often been afraid. But I would not give in to it. I simply acted as though I was not afraid and presently the fear disappeared." Fear is afraid itself and backs down when you stand up to it.

FEBRUARY

February 1 ------------------------------------

It is winter now and the snows can come. It's good to warm yourself before a roaring fire on a winter's night. Lowell Thomas, in persuading me to take up cross-country skiing, said, "To glide quietly on the snow into a grove of great old trees, their bare branches lifted to a cloudless blue sky, and to listen to the palpable silence, is to live in depth." In return, I quoted to him Thomas Carlyle's thoughtful line, "Silence is the element in which great things fashion themselves together."

February 2 ------------------------------------

I once knew an extraordinarily successful salesman who told me that every morning he says aloud, three times, "I believe, I believe, I believe." "You believe in what?" I asked. "In God, in Jesus, and in the life God gave me," he declared.

February 3 ------------------------------------

At dinner with some Chinese friends, the conversation turned to the stress and tension so prevalent today. "Bad way to live," said an aged man present. "Tension is foolish. Always take an emergency leisurely." "Who said that?" I asked. "I did," he replied with a smile, "and, if you quote it, just say an old Chinese philosopher said it." Well, it is sound philosophy. "Always take an emergency leisurely."

February 4

To have great days, it helps to be a tough-minded optimist. Tough doesn't mean swaggering, sneering, hard-boiled. The dictionary definition is a masterpiece: "Tough—having the quality of being strong or firm in texture, but flexible; yielding to force without breaking, capable of resisting great strain without coming apart." And Webster defines optimism as "the doctrine that the goods of life overbalance the pain and evil of it, to minimize adverse aspects, conditions, and possibilities, or anticipate the best possible outcome; a cheerful and hopeful temperament."

February 5

My wife, Ruth, and I have a friend, a charming lady down South, who has the typical accent and a big smile. It is her habit every morning, rain or shine, to fling open her front door and say aloud: "Hello there. Good morning." She explains: "Oh, I love the morning. It brings me the most wonderful surprises and gifts and opportunities." Naturally, she has a great day every day.

February 6

Henry Ford was once asked where his ideas came from. There was a saucer on his desk. He flipped it upside down, tapped the bottom, and said: "You know that atmospheric pressure is hitting this object at fourteen pounds per square inch. You can't see it or feel it, but you know it is happening. It's that way with ideas. The air is full of them. They are knocking you on the head. You only have to know what you want, then forget it and go about your business. Suddenly the idea will come through. It was there all the time."

February 7

To maintain a happy spirit, and to do so come what may, is to make sure of a great day every day. Wise old Shakespeare tells us that "a light heart lives long." It seems that a happy spirit is a tonic for long life. Seneca, the old Roman, also a thinker rich in wisdom, sagely observed, "It is indeed foolish to be unhappy now because you may be unhappy at some future time."

February 8

Someone tells the story of when, down in North Carolina, a man asked a weather-beaten mountaineer how he was feeling. "It's like this," drawled the man from the hills after a few seconds of silence. "I'm still kickin', but I ain't raisin' any dust." When you get right down to it, if we just keep on kickin', there is always hope.

February 9

How many unhappy people suffer the mental paralysis of fear, self-doubt, inferiority, and inadequacy! Dark thoughts blind them to the possible outcomes which the mind is well able to produce. But optimism infuses the mind with confidence and builds up belief in oneself. Result? The revitalized mind, newly energized, comes to grips with problems. Keep the paralysis of unhealthy thoughts out of that incomparable instrument, your mind.

February 10 —————————————————

Optimism is a philosophy based on the belief that basically life is good, that, in the long run, the good in life overbalances the evil. Also that, in every difficulty, every pain, there is some inherent good. And the optimist means to find the good. No one ever lived a truly upbeat life without optimism working in his mind.

February 11 —————————————————

In Tokyo I once met another American, an inspiring man, from Pennsylvania. Crippled from some form of paralysis, he was on an around-the-world journey in a wheelchair, getting a huge kick out of all his experiences. I commented that nothing seemed to get him down. His reply was a classic: "It's only my legs that are paralyzed. The paralysis never got into my mind."

February 12 —————————————————

Practice loving people. It is true that this requires effort and continued practice, for some are not very lovable, or so it seems—with emphasis upon "seems." Every person has lovable qualities when you really learn to know him.

February 13

A sure way to a great day is to have enthusiasm. It contains a tremendous power to produce vitality, vigor, joyousness. So great is enthusiasm as a positive motivational force that it surmounts adversity and difficulty and, moreover, if cultivated, does not run down. It keeps one going strong even when the going is tough. It may even slow down the aging process for, as Henry Thoreau said, "None are so old as those who have outlived enthusiasm."

February 14

On Valentine's Day I might call your attention to the law called the law of attraction—like attracts like. If you constantly send out negative thoughts, you tend to draw back negative results to yourself. This is as true as the law that lifts the tide. But a person who sends out positive thoughts activates the world around him positively and draws back to himself positive results.

February 15

A lifetime on this wonderful and exciting earth doesn't last very long. It is here today and gone tomorrow, so thank God every day for it. Life is good when you treat it right. Love life and it will love you back.

February 16

Life is not always gentle—far from it. From time to time, it will hand you disappointment, grief, loss, or formidable difficulty, often when least expected. But never forget you can surmount the worst it brings, keep on going, and make your way up again. You will find that you are stronger and maybe even better off for having had some tough experiences.

February 17 ————————————————

We are so accustomed to being alive that we take it for granted. The thrill and wonder of it doesn't often occur to us. Do you ever get up in the morning and look out the window, or go to the door and breathe in the fresh air, and go back in and say to your spouse, "Isn't it great to be alive?" Life is such a tremendous privilege, so exciting, that it is a cause for constant thanksgiving.

February 18 ————————————————

My old friend and associate, the famous psychiatrist Dr. Smiley Blanton, used to say: "No matter what has happened to a person, that individual still has within vast undamaged areas. Nature always tries to repair, so don't become dismayed, certainly never be discouraged, when you suffer a blow."

February 19 ————————————————

My mother used to tell me: "As you go through life, doors will sometimes shut in your face. But don't let that discourage you. Rather welcome it—for that is the way you are pointed to the open door, the right opening for you."

February 20 ━━━━━━━━━━━━━━━━━━━━━━━━

Here is a good mental diet:

1. *Think no ill about anyone.*
2. *Put the best possible construction upon everyone's actions.*
3. *Send out a kindly thought toward any person antagonistic to you.*
4. *Think hopefully at all times.*
5. *See only the best happening.*

February 21 ━━━━━━━━━━━━━━━━━━━━━━

When life hands you a lemon, make lemonade. Remember, there is no situation so completely hopeless that something constructive cannot be done about it. When faced with a minus, ask yourself what you can do to make it a plus. A person practicing this attitude will extract undreamed-of outcomes from the most unpromising situations. Realize that there are no hopeless situations; there are only people who take hopeless attitudes.

February 22 ━━━━━━━━━━━━━━━━━━━━━━━

I remember a sign I once saw on an office wall: "He who stumbles twice on the same stone deserves to break his neck." That may be rather harshly stated but it emphasizes the truth that a wise person does not get bogged down in a psychology of mistakes or allow errors to accumulate in the mind. When you make a mistake, take corrective action. Once is enough.

February 23 ━━━━━━━━━━━━━━━━━━━━━━━

I knew a man who was always saying, "You know, I've half a mind to do this or that." I told him, "Charley, you're a half-a-minder. Everything you think of doing, you have only half a mind to do. No one ever got anywhere with only half a mind." Success requires giving the whole self, the whole mind. Charley became an all-outer and achieved all-out success.

February 24 ━━━━━━━━━━━━━━━━━━━━━━━

Success in any business, or for that matter in any kind of undertaking, is determined by six simple words: *find a need and fill it*. In fact, these six words can be equated with practically every successful enterprise or personal career.

February 25 ━━━━━━━━━━━━━━━━━━━━━━━

Champions are made by playing their best game today, then tomorrow, and then the next day. Life, too, must be lived well one day at a time every day. And, in both sports and living, success is the result of a succession of more good days than bad ones.

February 26 ━━━━━━━━━━━━━━━━━━━━━━━

Start preparing for a happy old age when you are young— for, at seventy, you will be as you are at thirty, only more so. If you are tight with money at thirty, you will be a miser at seventy. If you talk a lot at thirty, you will be a windbag at seventy. if you are kind and thoughtful at thirty, you will be lovable at seventy.

February 27 ━━━━━━━━━━━━━━━━━━━━━━━

A lightweight football player used a law of physics to overcome his small size against the giants. Knowing that momentum is the product of mass and velocity, he took to projecting himself at high speed against opponents. This bulletlike human being hurled himself against bigger men. He knocked them over like pins in a bowling alley. This is good strategy to use on big problems.

February 28 ━━━━━━━━━━━━━━━━━━━━━━━

If you worry, you are a worrier because your mind is saturated with worry thoughts. To counteract these, mark every passage in your Bible that speaks of faith, hope, and courage. Commit each to memory until these spiritual thoughts saturate the mind.

February 29 ━━━━━━━━━━━━━━━━━━━━━━━

This is the extra day we have every four years. Just think, if you live for eighty years, you will have twenty priceless additional days of life. On this one day in Leap Year, God gives us an extra chance at living. Perhaps we should do something special with it, something like making some- one's life a bit happier, healing a breach, or offering prayers for persons who are having a hard time of it.

MARCH

March 1 ━━━━━━━━━━━━━━━━━━━━━━━━━━━━━━

Every month is a new beginning. So is every new day.
Perhaps that is why God brings down the curtain of night—to
blot out the day that is gone. All of your yesterdays ended
last night. It makes no difference how long you've been
alive, they're all ended. This day is absolutely new. You've
never lived it before. What an opportunity!

March 2 ━━━━━━━━━━━━━━━━━━━━━━━━━━━━━━

Harry Truman once said, "If you're afraid of getting burned,
better stay out of the kitchen." If you are going to fight for
principles and convictions, you can hardly avoid a rough
time now and then. Never weaken or back down—as all of
us feel like doing at times. If we yield to that temptation,
life may be easier but it certainly will be less interesting.

March 3 ━━━━━━━━━━━━━━━━━━━━━━━━━━━━━━

A man said that for years he had been extremely nervous
but had finally "practiced" his way out of that condition.

The word *practiced* makes sense, for it is certain that no real attainment comes without practice.

March 4 ━━━━━━━━━━━━━━━━━━━━━━━━

Learn what you can from the beating you have taken. Then move confidently on to the next opportunity. Accept defeat supinely and you're through. Come back at it with all you've got and you've got plenty. You will win with the *never settle for defeat* attitude.

March 5 ━━━━━━━━━━━━━━━━━━━━━━━━

There is one way to avoid criticism: Never do anything, never amount to anything. Never get your head above the crowd so that the jealous will notice and attack you. Criticism is a sign that your personality has some force.

March 6 ━━━━━━━━━━━━━━━━━━━━━━━━

Churchgoing can be exciting. A westerner once told me, after a Sunday service, "I came out of church so thrilled, I felt I could throw a lasso around the moon."

March 7 ━━━━━━━━━━━━━━━━━━━━━━━━

Almighty God freely bestows the good things in this world in proportion to a person's mental readiness to receive. An individual coming to the divine storehouse with a teaspoon, thinking "lack," will receive only a teaspoonful. Another more positive and believing person coming forward confidently with a gallon container will receive a gallon of life's blessing. We can only receive that which we expect according to our faith. So think big.

March 8

Your greatest ability is the power to choose. By the power of choice, you can make your life creative or you can destroy it. Every day we make many choices. Some are seemingly small, but no choice is altogether insignificant, for upon the most seemingly unimportant choice may ultimately depend the outcome of your life. History, they say, often turns on small hinges. That is also true of people's lives.

March 9

The sense of God's presence steadies us, gives us an anchor in the storm, and provides a reservoir of personal power. If you live with God as a friend, He will become so real that He will be your sturdy companion day and night. Then, even when the going is difficult, your heart can be happy within, for you have Him with you.

March 10

"Why can't we have a world that's peaceful and quiet?" a man asked. I told him about an old Irish friend who said there was a tradition in northern Ireland that, when there is trouble on the earth, it means there's movement in heaven. And this wise old man told me, "I always rejoice when there's lots of conflict and upset on the earth, because I know that out of this turmoil a movement in heaven will bring something good."

March 11

Don't talk trouble. It only activates more of it. Talk life up, not down. Talking tends to create or destroy, for it puts the immense power of thought to work along the lines indicated by the talk. Always remember Ralph Waldo Emerson's warning that a word is alive. By repeated use, it can either build or tear down.

March 12

A business executive had three boxes on his desk labeled INCOMING, OUTGOING, and UNDECIDED. The latter usually contained the most papers. Then he added a fourth box which he labeled WITH GOD ALL THINGS ARE POSSIBLE. When faced with a particularly tough problem he would prepare a memo and toss it into this box. Then he would go on to other matters, believing that at the proper time he would receive God's guidance. The six-word affirmation on the box positivized the man's attitude and kept reminding him that possibilities existed. Even though a decision was not clear, this thinking challenged him to discern and finally realize those possibilities.

March 13

A formula for self-improvement is to first decide specifically what particular characteristic you desire to possess and then hold that image firmly in consciousness. Second, develop that image by acting as if you actually possessed the desired characteristic. Third, believe and repeatedly affirm that you are in the process of self-creating and the quality you wish to develop.

March 14

People often kill their happiness and their success in life by their tongues. They explode, say a mean thing, write a sharp letter, and the evil is done. And, sadly, the real victim is not the other person but oneself.

March 15

The writer William A. Ward formulated a plan for successful achievement. He called it the "8 P Plan" and it goes like this: Plan Purposefully, Prepare Prayerfully, Proceed Positively, Pursue Persistently.

March 16

The biblical advice "Do not let the sun go down on your anger" is psychologically sound. Anger can accumulate to the exploding point and must be emptied out every night. Drain off the anger content that may be seething in your mind by forgiving everybody. And practice the art of forgetting.

March 17

We love those who make us believe in ourselves. "This above all," Shakespeare wrote, "to thine own self be true, And it must follow, as the night the day, Thou canst not then be false to any man."

March 18 ━━━━━━━━━━━━━━━━━━━━━━━━

There is only one person with whom to compete and that is yourself. Keep aiming to surpass your own best performance and ever strive to reach higher levels. If you are always measuring yourself against some other person, resentment and antipathy are bound to develop within your mind. Then tension mounts, you are thrown off your timing, and poorer performance results. Remember Thomas Edison's challenge: "There is a better way. Find it."

March 19 ━━━━━━━━━━━━━━━━━━━━━━━━

The average person uses only a small fraction of his potential abilities. Some authorities estimate that this is somewhere around ten percent of capacity. One reason is that we do not devote enough attention and time to deliberate, systematic development of our personalities. And another is that we frustrate ourselves with self-imposed limitations. Try to reach your full potential.

March 20 ━━━━━━━━━━━━━━━━━━━━━━━━

After a heated struggle in the U.S. House of Representatives over an important bill, an older congressman, Madden, approached a junior representative whose support of the bill had obviously been gained by questionable means. "Son," he asked, "why did you vote as you did?" "I had to," the young man answered. "I was under very great pressure." The older man put his hand on his younger colleague's shoulder. "But boy," he asked, "where are your inner braces?" Faith can brace us against pressure.

SPRING.

URING LATE MARCH, SPRING IS SUPPOSED TO APPEAR, at least tentatively. Officially, March 21 is the first day of spring, but it just could be that, on this date, the great March winds are blowing and sighing around the house and snow is in the air. Actually, long experience indicates that spring comes when it comes and only then.

Crocuses are usually up by late March. On our place, we have planted them around the base of our huge and ancient maples as well as along the driveways. They are optimistic, as flowers go, for they will push up from the ground in what seems a most inauspicious climate, and, if the cold is as sometimes occurs, more January-like, they hang their heads disconsolately. But, at the first opportunity, they are sprightly again and add great charm to springtime over the several weeks that they are in bloom.

Then along come hyacinths, jonquils, and daffodils. I like them because they are not only optimistic that spring has really come but they also reveal an indomitability that humans might well emulate.

One spring, all was bright and beautiful. The balmy air, so definitely associated with springlike days, was softly engaging. The flowers exuded the confidence that finally they had it made. Spring was here at last. But, during an April night, someone must have gotten the calendar mixed up. There was a throwback to the wild and gusty winds of March. Then the snow began falling thick and fast. Big winter flakes they were and, when chilly morning came, a real winter snow lay six inches deep upon the ground, including the flower beds. The hyacinths stood pretty straight, considering the weight of the snow, but the jonquils and daffodils bent over as if it was all too much for them.

But, having lived through many a springtime in our part of the country, we were not too much concerned. And, sure enough, the next day came a warm wind, the snow melted and, behold, the flowers perked up, took a wondering look around, then stood tall and straight and went about their business of blooming and being beautiful. All of which was a reminder of the rebound quality built into nature. I wonder if it is not also built into human nature. Perhaps one function of flowers and trees is to remind us that we, too, have a comeback quality.

I've seen trees devastated by winter storms—branches broken and hurled to the ground, tops apparently ruined. Then comes spring with God's healing touch; a multitude of leaves hides the hurt and, after a couple of springtimes, it is hard to find the damage, so great is a tree's repair power. Similarly, people are hurt. Some never recover but perhaps most do for they, like the trees, have an astounding ability to repair their hurts. They do, after all, have the same Healer.

March 21

At long last, every one of us draws to himself exactly what he is. If you want to know what life is going to bring you, all you need to do is to analyze yourself.

March 22

An incredible goodness is operating in your behalf. Confidently receive God's abundant blessings. Think abundance, prosperity, and the best of everything. Expect great things to happen. God wants to give you every good thing. Do not hinder His generosity by disbelief.

March 23

Standing by my mother's tombstone, I saw it for what it was—a place where only mortal remains lay. Her mortal body was only a coat laid aside because the wearer needed it no longer. But she, that gloriously lovely spirit, was not there. I walked out of the cemetery and rarely return—for she is not there. She is with her loved ones for always. "Why seek ye the living among the dead?" (Luke 24:5). You can depend upon the reliability of Christ. He would not let us believe and hold convictions so sacred unless they were true.

March 24

If you want a desirable quality in your life, let me remind you to use the "as if" principle—act *as if* you already have it. As you act and persevere in acting, so you tend to become. Try it—it's powerful and it works. If one acts as if God were with him, if he talks to God as if God were listening to him, in due course, he becomes very sure of God. You then know that God is with you always as He said He would be. And you know He is listening to your prayers.

March 25

Every human being needs to have a quiet center within his mind. You don't need to worry about confusion if you have inner quietness from which to handle it. And you can achieve this. You can learn to have a bit of God's great silence in your mind and heart.

March 26

We human beings often engage in the tragic process of mentally building up difficulties to overwhelming size and thus become afraid of them. We convince ourselves that we are defeated before we start and build a case for not trying. This is the time to release the sleeping giant within you. Then you become the great person you have it in you to be. You win victories instead of suffering defeats.

March 27

Most of us have no adequate conception of our inherent powers and abilities. At heart, we underestimate ourselves. We do not really believe in ourselves and for that reason remain weak, ineffectual, even impotent, when we could be strong, dominant, victorious. An old cobbler in Edinburgh was in the habit of beginning each day with the prayer, "O Lord, give me a high opinion of myself." Not a bad idea!

March 28 ---------------------------------------

Be yourself. Being a slave to conformity is one of the most fundamental of all dishonesties. When we reject our specialness, water down our God-given individuality and uniqueness, we begin to lose our freedom. The conformist is in no way a free man. He has to follow the herd. We need more "characters" among us, who do not weakly conform to standardized ways of behaving, people not afraid to be "different." Men and women who accomplish the most in this world are almost always "characters" in the sense that they are not afraid to be themselves regardless of what fashion or the "in" attitude dictates.

March 29 ---------------------------------------

Talk, actually speak, to the health forces within yourself. Summon them to your aid. Every day, strongly encourage God's health forces; restimulate them to creative action within your total being. Standing straight and tall, say: "I affirm the presence within me of God's recreative forces. I hereby yield myself in confidence to their health-giving effects. I affirm that the life force is renewing me now. I thank God, the Creator, but also the Re-Creator, now making me new."

March 30 ---------------------------------------

Make no mistake about it: any kind of dishonesty cripples, and the first thing you lose is freedom. One has to lie to cover up and soon becomes entangled in lies. An entangled person cannot be free. The honest person is the free person.

March 31 --

At some time during every day, I find it good to observe a period of absolute quiet, for there is healing power in silence. To find this power, do not talk; do not do anything; throw the mind into neutral; keep the body still; maintain complete silence. This is the practice of creative quiet.

APRIL

April 1 ————————————————

"Whether you *think* you can or *think* you can't—you are right," said Henry Ford.

April 2 ————————————————

That which we constantly affirm has the tendency to take over in our thoughts and to produce changed attitudes. A simple affirmation repeated three times every morning—such as "I am alive. Life is good. God is with me. I am going to have a wonderful day"—produces the results imaged.

April 3 ————————————————

The Bible puts it this way: "For as he thinketh in his heart, so is he" (Proverbs 23:7). Perhaps it might also be put this way: Think right to make things go right.

April 4 ━━━━━━━━━━━━━━━━━━━━━━━━━━━━━━━━

Workmen building the Panama Canal had been digging and excavating the big ditch for a long time. Just as they thought it was finished, there was a huge landslide and much of the dirt taken out fell back in again. The man in charge dashed up to the boss, General Goethals, and exclaimed: "It's terrible! Terrible! All the dirt's back in again! What shall we do?" Goethals said calmly, "Dig it out again." What else was there to do?

April 5 ━━━━━━━━━━━━━━━━━━━━━━━━━━━━━━━━

Louisa May Alcott was told by an editor that she would never be able to write anything that would have popular appeal. A music teacher told Enrico Caruso: "You can't sing. You have no voice at all." And a teacher warned a boy named Thomas A. Edison that he was too stupid to pursue a scientific education! Never let anyone shunt you off from the main line of your aspirations.

April 6 ━━━━━━━━━━━━━━━━━━━━━━━━━━━━━━━━

A fair amount of caution is sensible. Only a fool would be without it. But to listen to one's fears when seeking guidance is quite another matter. Consider cautiously, but take counsel from your beliefs, not your fears—and you will average out a lot better in life.

April 7 ━━━━━━━━━━━━━━━━━━━━━━━━━━━━━━━━

It isn't necessary or perhaps even good to have everyone like you. That idea can make you the worst kind of a mollycoddle. You will be spineless, uninteresting, lacking in character. Perhaps the greatest compliment ever paid President Grover Cleveland was when he was put in nomination before the Democratic Convention and the orator who presented his name said, "We love him for the enemies he has made."

April 8

One of the problems of our day is how to counteract the effects on the younger generation of a civilization dedicated to the pursuit of luxury and the avoidance of effort. A hundred years ago, there was kindling to be chopped, water to be carried, animals to be fed. But not anymore. We are in danger of robbing our children of one of their greatest heritages: that of struggle.

April 9

You never need to settle for what you are. You can be a new person. I've seen people change—defeated people become victorious, dull people become excited, real people experience marvelous change. We were not merely created: we can be re-created.

April 10

The more I see of people the more I'm impressed by their astounding ability to meet tough situations. And their ability to rebound is fantastic. There is a built-in comeback power in you that should never be underestimated.

April 11

In my youth, I heard a great speaker say, "You can become strongest in your weakest place." As in welding, the broken point becomes strongest when heat is applied. So thought and intensity of faith can weld the weak spots in personality into great strength. It's amazing what a person can creatively do with his own self.

April 12

Never run yourself down. Believe in yourself, esteem yourself not with egotism but with humble, realistic self-confidence. Stop brooding over the past. Drop the post-mortems. Live enthusiastically. Starting today, make the best you can of it. Give it all you've got and you will find that to be plenty.

April 13

When you have failed, your first step is to forget. The second is never to settle for it; never accept a failure. Then go right back at it again. Extract what know-how you can. Never say: "Well, I failed. That means I can't do it. I'll not try it anymore." That will develop the failure psychology in you so that you will become a failure person. Ask God's guidance about how to do the thing better the next time and keep right at it until you become a success person.

April 14

Many people suffering from unresolved fear find release and relief through the practice of courage and confidence.

These two positive mental attitudes—courage and confidence—banish fear; they make wonderful things happen. Yet all three—confidence, courage, fear—result from the kind of thoughts we think. The mental climate a person creates determines whether he will have confidence even when things seem hopeless and have courage even when apprehensive factors appear. Think courage, act with courage. Image yourself as confident. Act with confidence. As you think, act, and image, so shall you become.

April 15

When asked to explain his calm indifference to criticism a friend asked: "What happens when someone points a finger at you? Point your finger at me now." Nonplussed, I leveled my forefinger at him. "Now, who are your other three fingers pointing at?" "Why, they are pointing at me!" I exclaimed. "That's right," he concluded triumphantly. "So I win over a critic three to one!"

April 16

Waking up creatively every morning is an important skill in having a good day. It can be cultivated and developed so effectively that you can guarantee to yourself a good day, all day every day. As you arise in the morning, mentally picture the good day you want and confidently expect it. Picture it clearly in your mind. Strongly affirm the good day ahead. Then proceed to make it so.

April 17

Inscribed on a sundial on the Mount Holyoke College campus are these words: "To larger sight, the rim of shadow is the line of light." Perhaps death is only a momentary rim of shadow. Behind it, waiting, is the radiance of eternal life, the greatest days of all.

April 18

Watch out for defeat psychology. An experience in which you don't make out too well can shake your confidence in yourself; and, if you do not promptly make another try, defeat psychology can take hold and freeze you mentally. So, when you fall flat, pick yourself up fast and go right on to the next challenge. Don't give failure time to develop in your consciousness.

April 19

The most vital, creative, and positive thoughts are those stated in the Bible. Its words are alive and form powerful thought processes. The Bible itself states what its inspired words will do: "If ye abide in me, and my words abide in you, ye shall ask what ye will, and it shall be done unto you" (John 15:7).

April 20

Difficulties can be and often are blessings in disguise. Horace, the great Roman, said, "Difficulties elicit talents that in more fortunate circumstances would lie dormant." And Disraeli wrote, "Difficulties constitute the best education in this life."

April 21

When faced with great difficulties, hold clearly and tenaciously in your mind the thought that, with God's help, you can marshal your powers of concentration, reason, self-discipline, and imagination. And keep on believing that you actually do have the power to beat back circumstance. In so doing, you are bound to win.

April 22

A successful businesswoman commits every day to God. As a result of this practice, she says that nothing can be a disappointment because whatever happens is according to His plan and will. It changes disappointment to *His* appointment.

April 23

I have watched many star athletes. Looking back at the men who were consistently good—Ty Cobb, Lou Gehrig, Joe DiMaggio, Roger Hornsby, Duke Snyder—there was one quality possessed by all of them: *enthusiasm*. That spirit helped these men boost their batting averages to become the greatest performers in baseball history. It can help you.

April 24

On a classroom wall of my boyhood hung a picture showing a lonely beach with the tide out and a boat stranded on the sand. Few things look more depressing than a boat left high and dry by receding water. The inscription under the picture said, "Remember, the tide always comes back." There is ebb and flow in the vicissitudes of human life. When everything goes against you and it seems you can hold on no longer, never give up. The tide will turn.

April 25

In Kyoto there is a shrine famous for its stone garden. For centuries, fifteen stones of different shapes and sizes have been resting in a garden of carefully raked sand. By tradition, the stones represent the fifteen basic problems of mankind—every person names his or her own. But all the stones cannot be seen at the same time. The message I take away from the enigmatic stones at Kyoto is that no one can or should try to contemplate, much less solve, all his problems at once. People should instead make a deliberate mental effort to block out all their problems except one, and concentrate on solving that one—this way there is more mental strength to apply.

April 26

All actions, good or bad, start somewhere. They are best controlled at the start. If you stop the thought that leads to a dishonest action, you will block off the action itself.

April 27

The Kingdom of God is within you—within every man. It is God's gift to all humanity—available for the asking.

April 28 ————————————————————————

Twice he had failed in business—once during a depression
and again when a partner ruined him. Twice he started
over. Twice he was forced to sell out and work his way
out of debt. But did it faze him? Not at all. "A failure is
just the reverse side of success," he said. "With God's
help, I find you can always turn things around. I have faith
in God and faith in myself."

April 29 ————————————————————————

If you do not like a person, or he you, and you do
something for him, it can sometimes increase his dislike
because it puts him under obligation to you. He may even
regard your action as patronizing. But if you encourage
him to do something for you, he will feel complimented
despite himself and his good opinion of you will increase,
for you have shown that you respect his ability. You have
treated his ego with esteem.

April 30 ————————————————————————

A friend, Harry, loved dogs, especially a favorite, "Whiskers," who always went everywhere with him. Once Harry
had to go to a nearby town on some business. He wrote to
a hotel asking if he could bring his dog with him. The
reply was:

Dear Sir:
By all means bring your dog Whiskers along. Dogs
rate high in this hotel. Never have I had to eject an
unruly dog in the middle of the night. Never has a

dog gotten drunk and messed up my furniture. I have never had a dog go to sleep and set the mattress on fire with a lighted cigarette. Never has a dog made drinking-glass rings on my dressers. I have never yet found a towel or an ashtray in a dog's suitcase. So bring your dog along.

P.S. You can come, too, if the dog will vouch for you.

MAY

May 1 _____

I had made a speech to a large and friendly crowd. My cousin Philip Henderson heard me. Afterwards, he said: "You were not up to your best. It just wasn't good enough. You didn't give it all you've got. You coasted, you only wanted to get by. You must always do your top best, nothing else." It was a wise appraisal from one who loved me with the kind of love that gives it to you straight to make you be your best self.

May 2 _____

A friend has six gems of wisdom which he repeats almost every day. The first is from Cicero: "To live long, live slowly." The second is from Confucius: "The way of a superior man is threefold: virtuous, he is therefore free from anxiety; wise, he is therefore free from perplexity; bold, he is therefore free from fear." The third is from Robert Louis Stevenson: "Sit loosely in the saddle of life." The fourth, Saint Theresa's famous words: "Let nothing disturb you; let nothing frighten you. Everything passes except God; God alone is sufficient." And from

Isaiah, ". . . in quietness and in confidence shall be your strength" (Isaiah 30:15). Then finally, and most importantly, the words of Jesus: ". . . my peace I give unto you: not as the world giveth, give I unto you. Let not your heart be troubled, neither let it be afraid" (John 14:27).

May 3

Charles F. Kettering, the famous engineer, said: "I am not interested in the past. I am only interested in the future, for that is where I expect to spend the rest of my life!"

May 4

Once, in a restaurant, Henry Ford was asked, "Who is your best friend?" Ford thought for a moment, then took out his pen and wrote in large letters on the tablecloth, "He is your best friend who brings out of you the best that is in you."

May 5

Built into you is the inner fortitude and strength to stand up to things—to anything. The best lightning rod for your own protection is your own spine. That means, stand up straight and handle difficulties with faith in yourself.

May 6

A family holds a yearly "unhappy-thought burning." Each person drops into an urn pieces of paper on which they have written things they want to forget. They watch their unhappy thoughts burn and curl into ashes. This act helps them forget.

May 7

General Stonewall Jackson was approached by a timorous subordinate general who admitted grave doubts about a planned military sortie. "General Jackson," he said, "I'm afraid of this. I fear we can't quite carry it off." Jackson replied, "General, never take counsel of your fears."

May 8

A physician tells of a patient who died of "grudgitis"—a long-held hatred of another person. It is healthy to get rid of grudges; they seldom hurt the other person but they can make the holder sick.

May 9

My father, Charles Clifford Peale, often said to me, and indeed it was one of the last things he said: "I have always believed in you. You have never failed me. Remember, the Peales never quit." While I have not always lived up to my father's statement, one thing is sure—it has always helped when I begin to weaken.

May 10

There is only one power greater than fear, and that is faith. When fear comes to your mind, immediately counter it with an affirmation of faith. Think positively, visualize achievement. Never doubt. Always think faith.

May 11

Never settle for a failure. To do so is a serious blow to self-confidence. When an acrobat fails, he tries again, and, in fact, will keep the audience waiting for minutes, if necessary, until he completes his stunt successfully. He will not leave the stage until he has performed it. Otherwise he accepts into his consciousness the fact of failure so that the next time he performs he is afraid, is not sure he can do it and is, indeed, likely to fail.

May 12

The key phrase of failure is "if only." If only this hadn't happened! If only I had done differently. If only . . . if only! Shift the key words. Take "if only" out of the mental slot. Slide in a new phrase, image it locked into place in your mind. It can cancel out failure thinking. Instead of "if only," say "next time . . . next time . . . next time."

May 13

A man said: "I've been afraid, but not anymore, for now I've got the five Gs going for me: *Guidance:* God guides me in everything. *Grace:* God does for me what I cannot do for myself. *Guts:* Just plain man-sized courage. *Gumption:* Good old American common sense. And the greatest of all: *God.*"

May 14

In his book *The Unobstructed Universe*, Stewart Edward White suggests that when the blades of an electric fan are at rest, or moving slowly, you can't see through them. But when the fan is revolving at top speed you can see through all the points of the circle in which the blades are revolving, because they have been stepped up to a higher frequency. Is it not conceivable that around us now in this mysterious universe are those whom we have loved and lost for a while, and that we get glimpses through the barrier in rare moments when our spiritual frequency is at one with the higher frequency?

May 15

A friend, a famous baseball player, hit regularly in the neighborhood of .315. Early in the season I had listened on the radio through two innings of a game and was dismayed when he struck out. Meeting him later that day, I told him how sorry I was he had struck out. "Oh," he said, "I struck out again in the eighth inning." "Twice? What's happening to you?" I asked anxiously. "Nothing at all," he responded with unconcern. "I take comfort in the law of averages. To bat an average of .315 as I have been doing, one will strike out about ninety times a season. So today, when I fanned twice, it means I have only eighty-eight times more to strike out this season."

May 16

Some people feel they can change and improve their situation merely by moving from one place to another. "I'm tired of this job. My talent isn't being used. I'm not appreciated here. Think I'll look around." These statements are often born of illusion. People sometimes make them primarily because they are tired not only of the job but of themselves. Nothing is likely to change for them unless they first change their attitude. Then they won't require escape.

May 17 --

Empty pockets never held anyone back; it's only empty heads and empty hearts that do that.

May 18 --

Do the best you can, trust the Lord, serve Him, walk with God, love people, do your duty, be honorable and upright, live right, think right, and you will live at peace with yourself.

May 19 --

Every day, preferably about midafternoon, when energy lag usually comes, try repeating: ". . . in him we live, and move, and have our being . . ." (Acts 17:28), meanwhile visualizing yourself as plugged into the spiritual power line. Affirm that God's recreative energy is restoring strength and power and health to every part of your body, mind, and soul.

May 20 --

You can be made tired by your thoughts—thoughts of weariness, fear, anxiety, or resentment. But when you hold thoughts of hopefulness, confidence, positiveness, and good will, a constant flow of energy develops. Do not think tired thoughts. Think lively ones.

May 21

It is difficult to sustain concentrated, creative thinking. But we have the capacity to do so. As we keep thinking, never give up—solutions to problems will come. But the effort must be made and continued. As Leonardo da Vinci observed, God gives us everything "at the price of an effort."

May 22

I once asked President Dwight D. Eisenhower who was the greatest of all the great men he had known. His instant reply: "It wasn't a man. It was a woman—my mother. She had little schooling, but her educated mind, her wisdom, came from a lifelong study of the Bible. Often I have wished I could consult her. One night we were playing a card game, mother, my brothers, and I. Not with playing cards. It was Flinch—mother was straightlaced. But hands were dealt and I drew a bad one. I began to complain. " 'Put your cards down, boys,' Mother said. 'Dwight, this is just a friendly game in your home where you are loved. But, out in the world where there isn't so much love, you will be dealt many a bad hand. So you've got to learn to take the hands life deals you without complaining. Just play them out.' "

May 23

The controlled person is a powerful person. He who always keeps his head will get ahead. The number of people whose careers have been ruined through lack of emotional control is astonishing.

May 24

The mental and spiritual heat created by enthusiasm can burn off the apathy-failure factor in any personality and release hitherto unused, even unsuspected, personal power qualities. The president of a large corporation states: "If I am trying to decide between two men of fairly equal ability and one man has enthusiasm, I know he will go further than the other man, for enthusiasm acts as a self-releasing force." Enthusiasm is infectious. It carries all before it.

May 25

Physical death is a transitional step in the total life process. The soul, which does not die, having finished with the earthly body, moves to a higher level of life, where it grows under greatly enhanced circumstances.

May 26

Imagine yourself looking at all of your difficulties lined up like an army before you. As you face this army of discouragement, frustration, disappointment, hostility, and weakness, affirm, "If God be for us, who can be against us?" (Romans 8:31). Know that God is for you and His power is greater than all opposition. Visualize these enemies of your peace and happiness as retreating, giving way before God's power.

May 27

By always expecting the best, you are putting your whole heart and mind into what you want to accomplish. People are defeated in life not because of lack of ability but for lack of sustained expectation and wholeheartedness.

May 28

It is always well to remember that a lost battle or two or three does not mean the war is lost. With God's help, you can take any setback or defeat, muster your forces, and win out in the end.

May 29

In time of discouragement, it helps to take paper and pencil and add up all your assets—all that you have going for you. You will be astonished by what you have as you stop thinking about what you have not.

May 30

A physician told me he had seen people die, not because of organic trouble but because they had lost their enthusiasm, their will to live. Had they continued to possess the zest for life that enthusiasm gives, they could have overcome the physical problems that took their lives. Enthusiasm is an elixir of life.

So you've made a mistake. Who hasn't? But perhaps you feel it's a pretty serious one. I have always liked the following quotation from Grove Patterson, a famous editor:

> A boy . . . leaned against the railing of a bridge and watched the current of the river below. . . . Sometimes the current went more swiftly and again quite slowly, but always the river flowed on under the bridge. Watching the river that day, the boy made a discovery. It was not the discovery of a material thing, something he might put his hand upon. He could not even see it. He had discovered an idea. Quite suddenly, and yet quietly, he knew that everything in his life would someday pass under the bridge and be gone like water. . . . And he didn't worry unduly about his mistakes after that and he certainly didn't let them get him down, because it was water under the bridge.

JUNE

June 1

The big heart of faith can push the crushing circumstances of life wide apart. The positive mind is not limited. It has extra problem-solving power. People who have big hearts and big minds need not be afraid of what may come, for those hearts and minds determine the quality of the future.

June 2

God, who created us in the first place, continually re-creates. If we cooperate He will constantly fill us with new life, increased strength, and adequate power. You can have energy that never runs down if you image yourself as being constantly recreated.

June 3

One thing is sure—to live your life successfully you will need to overcome proneness to error or the mistake tendency. It is error that gets us into trouble. All of our failures and mistakes have been due to the mistake tendency. But rightness leads to right results and rightness is cultivatable.

June 4 ————————————————————————————

A. Harry Moore, a poor boy who became governor of New Jersey for three terms, had an early struggle to make a career. He often become discouraged and would say to his mother: "Mom, I'm discouraged. I want to do something and be somebody, but I just haven't got it in me. Besides, we have no money or influence." His mother's reply was blunt: "You've got plenty in you. All you need is God and gumption." It's a good formula: "God and gumption."

June 5 ————————————————————————————

When your feelings are hurt, what then? Immediately put some healing balm on that sore spot. Forgiveness is the best medicine. Open your mind completely and empty out all the grievances. Pour them out until not a vestige remains in your thoughts. Your hurts will heal quickly.

June 6 ————————————————————————————

To make the day good, visualize or image it in your mind as good. We become what we think. Our life's events, good or bad, are governed by our thoughts. Develop the habit of thinking good days and you will go a long way toward having good days.

June 7

Henry Thoreau, the American philosopher, upon awakening in the morning would lie abed telling himself all the good news he could think of: that he had a healthy body, that his mind was alert, that his work was interesting, that the future looked bright, that people trusted him. Presently, he arose to meet the day in a world filled with good things, good people, good opportunities.

June 8

Not every day can be an easy one, nor every day fully happy; but even a day of tough going and difficulty can be a good day. Robert Browning knew this when he wrote: "Meanwhile as the day wore on the trouble grew, Wherefrom I guessed there would be born a star."

June 9

Mentally picture your body as being perfect both in condition and in function. Do not visualize it as in decline or as deteriorating. Train yourself to stop looking for something to go wrong. Think positively about your physical self. Think health, not sickness. This is important, for mental images tend to reproduce themselves in fact.

June 10

On the dining room wall of a four-hundred-year-old inn in Saint Moritz, I read this inscription: "Just when you think everything is hopeless, a little ray of light comes from somewhere." Your mind may seem to be dark and hopeless. But Almighty God, the Creator, established hope in you, an unshatterable hope deep within yourself. If darkness has settled deeply in your mind, just open up your thoughts and let in that "little ray of light [that] comes from somewhere."

June 11

When Henry Ford, whom I like to quote, was seventy-five years old, he was asked the secret of his health and calm spirit. "Three rules," he answered. "I do not eat too much; I do not worry too much; and, if I do my best, I believe that what happens, happens for the best."

June 12

Members of a service club in one city went out to give a dollar to every person on the streets who looked happy. At the day's end, they had been able to give away only thirty-three dollars. Perhaps life in our cities is getting so impersonal that people feel insignificant and retreat into their shells and glare rather than smile. But a peaceful, happy face is a blessing to passersby and to oneself!

June 13

Ernest Hemingway wrote of a commander in the Spanish Civil War who "never knew when everything was lost and if it was, he would fight out of it." That is the way with people who have the quality of determination. They keep on going, no matter what. The hang-in-there attitude gives courage, strength, vitality, power. Somehow such people always seem to win through anything and everything.

June 14 ----------------------------------

Patient understanding is the secret of all human relationships.

June 15 ----------------------------------

The business card of a friend gives his name, company, address—all the usual information. On the reverse side is this message:

> *The Way to Happiness: Keep your heart free of hate. Keep your mind from worry. Live simply, expect little, give much. Fill your life with love. Scatter sunshine. Forget self, think of others. Do as you would be done by. Try this for a week and you will be surprised.*

June 16 ----------------------------------

We do not believe in immortality because we can prove it, but we try to prove it because we cannot help believing it. Indeed, the instinctive feeling that it is true is one of the deepest proofs of its truth. When God wishes to carry a point with His children, He plants the idea in their instincts. The instinct for immortality is of such universality that it can hardly be met with indifference by the universe. What we deeply long for, what we deeply feel, must surely reflect a basic fact of existence.

June 17 ----------------------------------

In a twisting little street in Kowloon, I passed a shop where tattooing was done. Pictured in the window were some suggestions: a mermaid, a flag, and the motto "Born to lose." I was so astonished by the latter that I entered the shop and asked the man if anyone ever had those words actually tattooed into his skin. "A few," he replied. But then he added a wise insight in broken English: "Before tattoo on body, tattoo on mind."

June 18 --

"We are saved by hope." This fragment of a passage from Romans 8:24 could mean many things. If we have hope in God, we are saved to eternity. If we have hope in life, we are saved from many a defeat and many a weakness. Nestle that passage up against your mind: "We are saved by hope."

June 19 --

When I joined the ranks of the grandfathers, I noted how times have changed. When I was a boy, grandfathers, to my young eyes, had one foot in the grave. But just take a look at grandfathers nowadays. They are a pretty sprightly lot. Indeed, they have to be to keep up with grandmothers.

June 20 --

Think joy, talk joy, practice joy, share joy, saturate your mind with joy, and you will have the time of your life today and every day all your life.

SUMMER

NOW COMES THE GOOD OLD SUMMERTIME. IT IS THAT time of year when nature, quietly but impressively, demonstrates its growing power. Trees have completed the old but ever amazing process of putting forth their thousands of leaves. I've always wondered how a tree knows when to adorn itself with leaves and how it does it. From the stark, bare branches of winter to the green leaves of summer is one of the astonishing miracles by which nature adds charm and beauty to our lives.

Flowers everywhere are adding to summer's festive character and the songs of birds joyously fill the air. Nests are in the trees and other nooks which father and mother birds have carefully selected. Balmy breezes blow softly and golden sunshine filters down through branches to fall gently upon clipped green grass. Corn is coming up in the fields. As the old saying goes, "It will be knee-high by the Fourth of July." Wind ripples caressingly over the growing wheat. At such times we may find ourselves repeating those familiar and famous lines from *The Vision of Sir Launfal* by James Russell Lowell:

> *And what is so rare as a day in June?*
> *Then, if ever, come perfect days;*
> *Then Heaven tries earth if it be in tune,*

And over it softly her warm ear lays;
Whether we look, or whether we listen,
We hear life murmur, or see it glisten;
Every clod feels a stir of might,
An instinct within it that reaches and towers,
And, groping blindly above it for light,
Climbs to a soul in grass and flowers.

Everything is perfection since good God, the Creator, designed and made it all. And He never did anything badly. But, with all respectful deference, I cannot help wondering, come every summer, just why the Lord thought it necessary to make mosquitoes and flying insects. Oh, I know it has to do with nature's balance and all that; still I must confess those creatures surely interfere with the perfect pleasures of summertime.

A few years ago, I purchased two old-fashioned rocking chairs from a firm down in Georgia that has been making them since before the Civil War, or if you're reading this down South, the "War Between the States." We have an 1830 house in Dutchess County, New York, just over the Connecticut line. It stands on a hill overlooking a great valley, its white pillars marking the wide front porch, which looks west toward the Hudson River.

Around the corner is a side porch looking over a valley southward. And the back porch off the kitchen looks over another valley into Connecticut. Here were placed these great rocking chairs. From this peaceful vantage, we look over a wide sweep of land, through great maples, across the valley to hills beyond.

On a warm summer afternoon or in the cool of twilight, I like to sit here with my wife, Ruth, rocking in perfect enjoyment until the mosquitoes surge in to attack all exposed parts and the gnats come en masse, buzzing and stinging. So, finally, I retreat inside the house thinking not the most kindly thoughts about summer. But actually, not even that affects the joy and glory of summer, the beautiful season at the fullness of the year.

Sometimes on a peaceful and lovely summer day I find myself reciting these lines of Robert W. Service:

> *The summer—no sweeter was ever;*
> *The sunshiny woods all athrill;*
> *The grayling aleap in the river;*
> *The bighorn asleep on the hill.*
>
> *The strong life that never knows harness;*
> *The wilds where the caribou call;*
> *The freshness, the freedom, the farness—*
> *O God! how I'm stuck on it all.*

From childhood to old age we love it, the good old summertime.

June 21 ━━━━━━━━━━━━━━━━━━━━━━━━━━━

How can a person gain promotion in a job? I suggest seven rules:

1. *Be intent only on doing your present job well.*
2. *Don't think about being promoted; think only of being efficient now.*
3. *Word hard.*
4. *Work early and late.*
5. *Study, study, study until you learn real know-how.*
6. *Work your head off.*
7. *Try not to have a heart attack.*

June 22 ━━━━━━━━━━━━━━━━━━━━━━━━━━━

During the Civil War, a man once stayed overnight at the White House in Washington. In the middle of the night he awakened suddenly and thought he heard Lincoln's voice, as though in pain, somewhere nearby. He jumped up, and went out into the dimly lit hall and, walking slowly in the direction of the voice, came to a door left ajar. Peering in, he beheld the lanky form of Lincoln prostrate on the floor in prayer, arms outstretched. Lincoln was humbly beseeching God to strengthen him against his sense of inadequacy. Lincoln knew he needed the great gift of God—"My peace I give unto you"—so he sought and prayed for it with all his mind and heart.

June 23 ━━━━━━━━━━━━━━━━━━━━━━━━━━━

You have vast undamaged areas within yourself! No matter what life has done, no matter what you have done; the renewal power is there within you. If you bring spiritual power to bear upon those undamaged areas, you can re-build life, no matter what has happened to it.

June 24 ---

Talking with Herbert Hoover in his later years, I asked him how he had been able to endure all the hostile criti-cism and hate that was heaped upon him during his last months in the White House. He said, "I'm a Quaker, you know . . ." and reminded me that Quakers are taught from childhood to practice and develop inner calm. "When you have peace at the center, the trying experiences cannot overwhelm you."

June 25 ---

God must surely be interested in our having good, strong, sound bodies—for does not the Bible tell us the body is the temple of the soul?

June 26 ---

When you have done your best and something frustrating happens, instead of being discouraged, examine the inter-ference. It may mean improvement. Thorvaldsen, the fa-mous Danish sculptor, looked with satisfaction on a finished figure of Christ he had made out of clay, with face looking toward heaven and arms extended upward. It was the imperious figure of a conqueror. That night, sea mist seeped into the studio, the clay relaxed, the head and arms dropped. Thorvaldsen was bitterly disappointed. But, as he studied the figure, something about it moved him deeply.

Now Christ looked down with love and compassion. This was a greater conception. That statue, *Come Unto Me*, became immortal.

June 27 ----------------------------------

Brother Lawrence, a saintly character of the Middle Ages, was a humble man, a cook and a great spiritual discoverer. His secret of the good life was the practice of the presence of God. He believed that always, at any hour of the day or night, in whatever circumstances or condition, the Lord is actually present.

June 28 ----------------------------------

The only way you can rid yourself of a thought or thought pattern is by displacement—by putting another thought in, by substitution or thought-switching. If you entertain in mind a defeat thought, a discouragement thought, a frustration thought, or any negative thought, practice thought substitution. Deliberately open the mind and substitute the contrary thought pattern, one positive in nature. Such thought conditioning can change your life.

June 29 ----------------------------------

Gloom drives prosperity away. Prosperity shies away from dark and negative thoughts, veering off from minds filled with pessimism and doubts. So think bright thoughts and attract prosperity. Note that the word *scarcity* is built upon the word *scare*. Be careful not to think scarcity and so scare prosperity away. Think plenty and stimulate abundance.

—●—●—●—●—●—●—●—●—●—●—●—●—●—●—

Here is a five-day mental diet. It's good for healthy-mindedness. It will help give you a great day every day.

FIRST DAY: *Think no ill about anybody—only good about everybody.*

SECOND DAY: *Put the best possible construction, the most favorable interpretation, on the behavior of everybody you encounter or have dealings with.*

THIRD DAY: *Send out kindly thoughts toward every person you contact or think of.*

FOURTH DAY: *Think hopefully about everything. Immediately cancel out any discouraging thought that comes to mind.*

FIFTH DAY: *Think of God's presence all day long.*

JULY

July 1

What is hope? Hope is wishing for a thing to come true—faith is believing that it will come true. Hope is wanting something so eagerly that, in spite of all evidence that you're not going to get it, you go right on expecting it. And the remarkable thing is that this very act of hoping produces a strength of its own.

July 2

There is a spiritual giant within each of us telling us we need not remain enslaved by weakness or victimized by frustrating limitations. The giant within you is always struggling to burst his way out of the prison you have made for him. Why not set him free today?

July 3

Thomas Edison is supposed to have made a curious remark which is fascinating: "The chief function of the body is to carry the brain around." That is to say, you are what you think and your life is determined by what goes on in your brain. The brain is the center of thought, memory, feeling, emotion, dreams, prayer, faith; in short, it is the creative and directing center of the entire person. The body may become old, feeble, suffer disability; but so long as the brain is clear and in working order, so long do you really live.

July 4 --

Winston Churchill once gave a talk to the boys of Harrow, his old school. He stressed the importance of believing they could win. "Never, never, never, never give in," he told them. Four times he said "never." Churchill gave those boys the basis of success: Never quit.

July 5 --

A positive thinker does not refuse to recognize the negative; he refuses to dwell on it. Positive thinking is a form of thought which habitually looks for the best results from the worst conditions.

July 6 --

The head of a university hospital once said, "When a person becomes ill he should send for his minister, priest, or rabbi as he sends for his doctor." That is to say, the sick may be helped in two ways: through the science of medicine and surgery, and through the effective use of faith and prayer.

July 7

There is no circumstance in your life where God will not stand with you and help you, no matter what the trouble may be. He understands all your problems, all your frustrations and disappointments. He sympathizes in your weaknesses. He loves you.

July 8

An old man appeared on a popular television program. He had received a prize for having won a contest. He stole the show with his exuberant spirit and quick wit. "It's easy to see," remarked the admiring master of ceremonies, "that you are a very happy man. What's the secret of being as happy as you are? Let us in on it." "Why, son," the old man answered, "it's as plain as the nose on your face. When I wake up in the morning, I have two choices. One is to be unhappy; the other is to be happy. And I want you to know, son, that I'm not as dumb as I may look. I'm smart enough to choose happiness. I just make up my mind to be happy . . . that's all there is to it."

July 9

A friend once had a problem that had been agitating his mind for days and to which he could not get an answer. He decided to practice "creative spiritual quietness." He went alone into a church and sat for an extended period in absolute silence. Presently, he began to be conditioned to quietness. Finally, he "dropped" his problem into a deep pool of mental and spiritual silence. He meditated upon God's peace rather than upon the specific details of the problem. This seemed to clarify his thinking and, before leaving that quiet place, an answer began to emerge which proved to be the right one.

July 10 ------------------------------------

A physician tells me that 35 to 50 percent of the ill are sick because they are basically unhappy. "Joy has significant therapeutic or healing value," he says, "whereas gloom and depression militate against creative life processes." Learn to live the joy way, for "a merry heart doeth good like a medicine" (Proverbs 17:22).

July 11 ------------------------------------

In this life, we must learn to develop the quality of urbane imperturbability. This is the ability to accept people as they are, and not let their annoying actions get under your skin. It will, in time, even get you to loving people.

July 12 ------------------------------------

The late Mrs. Thomas A. Edison told me that when her husband was dying he whispered to his physician, "It is very beautiful over there." Edison was a scientist, with a factual cast of mind. He never reported anything as fact until he saw it work. He would never have reported, "It is very beautiful over there," unless, having seen, he knew it to be true.

July 13 ------------------------------------

If a person habitually thinks optimistically and hopefully he activates life around him positively and thereby attracts to himself positive results. What you mentally project reproduces in kind. Positive thinking sets in motion positive and creative forces and success flows toward you.

July 14

Don't be an *if* thinker; be a *how* thinker. The *if* thinker mouths, "If only I'd had a break." The *how* thinker emphasizes the hows: "How do I compensate for this shortcoming?" or "How do I accomplish it?"

July 15

What are the essential factors in creative and exciting successful living? Number one is to be chief executive officer over your life and over yourself. When you feel life is pushing you around, or you are being pushed around by a variable self, you are not happy or effective. But when you become supervisor of your life, there is no joy in the world equal to it or to the excitement and satisfaction you will feel.

July 16

Deep within the individual is a vast reservoir of untapped power waiting to be used. No person can have the use of all this potential until he learns to know his or her own self. The trouble with many people who fail is that they go through life thinking and writing themselves off as ordinary, commonplace persons. Having no proper belief in themselves, they fail to utilize their talents. They live aimless and erratic lives very largely because they never realize what their lives really can be or what they can become.

July 17

One of the greatest things you will ever be able to say in your lifetime is this: "I have realized the potential that Almighty God put into me."

July 18

Life for most of us contains many tough and difficult problems; we need all the confidence and reassurance we can get. Nothing builds confidence and reassurance like a word of praise. Nothing restores our self-esteem and recharges our batteries like a little admiration. Why, then, needing appreciation ourselves so badly, do we deny it so often to others?

July 19

Practice changing critical attitudes toward your fellowmen. Get in the habit of looking for something to praise, something good to say. Once you start picking at people critically, you will find yourself criticizing everything they do. Reverse this mental attitude by finding something, however small, to praise in everyone. It will greatly add to your own happiness.

July 20

God answers prayer in three ways: *yes, no,* and *wait awhile.* If you receive a *no* answer, look for the lesson the *no* answer teaches. God sometimes shuts doors to lead you to the right open door. If you experience difficulty and hardship, perhaps it is because God wants to do something for you other than you expected or have yet experienced.

July 21

"Don't you know the world is full of problems?" asked the negative thinker. "But the world is also full of the overcoming of problems," replied the positive thinker.

July 22

Every last one of us possesses the power to live a truly wonderful life; yet we settle for being unhappy, when it isn't necessary. We should ask ourselves what we have done with the talents and abilities which God built into us. Every human being ought to look inside himself and thank the good Lord that he has unused strength he has never drawn on—and then start drawing on it.

July 23

Help others to overcome fear and worry and you gain greater power over these problems yourself. Every day think of yourself as living in companionship with Jesus Christ. If he actually walked by your side, you would not be worried or afraid. Say, "He is with me now." Repeat it every time you feel fear or begin to worry. Recommend the practice to others as I do to you. It works.

July 24

The world needs millions of acts of forgiveness and repentance to flush out hate, resentment, and bitterness.

July 25

What's wrong with having problems? The only people who have no problems are in cemeteries. Problems are a sign of life. So be glad you've got them. It means you are alive. The more problems you have, the more alive you are. If you have no problems, better get down on your knees and ask: "Lord, don't You trust me anymore? Give me some problems."

July 26

You need not fear if you know an action is right. Pray about it to be sure it's right, for if it isn't right it's wrong, and nothing wrong can turn out right. Knowing you are right, there is nothing in this world that can defeat you. It may go hard; you may receive blows. But God will not let you down. He will see you through. Know you are right, then fearlessly go ahead.

July 27

Having asked God for forgiveness, accept release, then truly forgive yourself and turn your back definitely on the matter. Fill your mind with hopeful, helpful, and positive thoughts. Have faith and go forward. "Forgetting those things which are behind, and reaching forth unto those things which are before" (Philippians 3:13).

July 28

The best way to deal with a problem is this: Write it down on a piece of paper. Study its component parts. Think it through. Then put it aside and think of God. Forget the problem. Think of God. The more you think of Him, the more He will put ideas into your mind when you pick up the problem again. You will get your answer. God answers. If you don't get it that first time, you will the second or the third. *Shift from the problem to God.*

July 29 ----------------------------------

Many of the world's finest Oriental rugs come from little villages in the Middle East, China, or India. These rugs are hand-produced by crews of men and boys under the direction of a master weaver. They work from the underside of the rug-to-be. It frequently happens that a weaver absentmindedly makes a mistake and introduces a color that is not according to the pattern. When this occurs, the master weaver, instead of having the work pulled out in order to correct the color sequence, will find some way to incorporate the mistake harmoniously into the overall pattern. In weaving our lives, we can learn to take unexpected difficulties and mistakes and weave them advantageously into the greater overall patterns of our lives. There is an inherent good in most difficulties.

July 30 ----------------------------------

If you will set aside a few minutes, ten or even five, to think about God and Christ, to confess your sins, to pray for those who have done wrong against you, and to ask for strength—and if you do this consistently day after day—a true faith will begin to send spiritual health and power through your personality.

Positive thinking is how you *think* about a problem. Enthusiasm is how you *feel* about a problem. The two together determine what you *do* about a problem.

AUGUST

August 1

Say to yourself every day, especially when things get dark and trouble stares you in the face, "I am a child of God." Asserting and affirming your divine origin will strengthen you and you will realize that whatsoever comes you have Someone watching over you and helping you. This practice will help you to have a great day every day.

August 2

My method for awakening is this: When I return to at least a semiconscious state after a night of sleep, while still lying in bed, I repeat this phrase from Psalm 139: "When I awake, I am still with thee" (verse 18). These words emphasize the greatest truth known to man—that we are not alone. Then, just before getting out of bed, I repeat that glorious old passage from Psalm 118: "This is the day which the Lord hath made; we will rejoice and be glad in it" (verse 24). He made this day to be a precious thing full of opportunity; He gives it to us. We must do something good with this day.

August 3

A prominent businessman whose daily schedule is packed to the limit, his responsibilities many and his activities widely diverse, always handles himself with impressive quietness. "I have learned to begin and end each day calmly," he says. "I repeat to myself this line from Isaiah: 'In quietness and in confidence shall be your strength' [Isaiah 30:15]. That is my secret."

August 4

Enthusiasm is no Pollyannish, sweetness-and-light, inborn and fortuitous concept. It is a strong, rugged mental attitude that is perhaps hard to achieve, difficult to maintain, but powerful—so powerful!

August 5

How do some people rise above calamities that leave others crushed in spirit, bitter and defeated? In the Book of Job we find a clue: "When he [God] giveth quietness, who then can make trouble?" (Job 34:29). The first essential for meeting misfortune sturdily is to achieve quietness, calmness, serenity at the center of yourself. Out of such quietness at the center arises simple gratitude—for the gift of life, for present blessings, for advantages and possibilities you do have. This thankfulness, in turn, opens doors to happiness and opportunity which otherwise remain closed.

August 6

A prayer for energy: Dear Lord, I need more energy and strength. I seem drained and tired. I do not seem to possess what it takes to do all that I must do. I know that the wrong kind of thoughts can make one tired. Change my thoughts that they may be in harmony with Your power. Keep me in close contact with You who are the Source of energy, energy that never runs down. I accept this strength and energy now. I thank you. Amen.

August 7

A long while ago, there was a man who had to hook up his wife's long dresses every day. They used to hook from top to bottom and he got tired of the job. It was most exasperating. He nearly lost his religion every time he did it. He is the fellow who developed the zipper. He met a situation with creativity.

August 8

To cure worry, spend fifteen minutes daily filling your mind full of God. Worry is just a very bad mental habit. You can change any habit with God's help. Start practicing faith, the number-one enemy of worry. Every morning say, "I believe," out loud, three times. Pray: "I place my life, my loved ones, my work in the Lord's hands. There is only good in Your hands. Amen."

August 9

While driving your car, if you become annoyed by impolite and careless actions on the part of another driver, instead of reacting in kind, remain affable and send up a sincere prayer for him. You can never know what pressures motivate him. Perhaps your prayer may reach his problem. One thing is sure, it will reach you.

August 10

Beneath the tension-agitated surface of our minds is the profound peace of the deeper mental levels. As the water beneath the surface of the ocean is deep and quiet, no matter how stormy the surface, so the mind is peaceful in its depths. Silence, practiced until you grow expert in its use, has the power to penetrate to that inner center of mind and soul where God's healing quietness may actually be experienced.

August 11

When you get discouraged, when you cannot seem to make it, there is one thing you cannot do without. It is that priceless ingredient of success called relentless effort. You just never give up, never quit.

August 12

"Let your requests be made known to God," says the Bible (Philippians 4:6). But it also says, "Your Father knows what you need before you ask Him" (Matthew 6:8). Ask for what you want but always be willing to take what God gives. It may prove better than what you ask for.

August 13

Have you ever noticed how people who master words and use them well, bringing out their beauty and employing their persuasiveness, are those who go far in life. One does not need be a great platform speaker. The fine choice of vocabulary in daily speech will mark one as different and of extra quality and in a quiet way that person will become a leader. Just think what wonderment is inherent in a combination of words.

August 14 ————————————————

You can reach any goal . . .

> **IF** *you know what the goal is;*
> **IF** *you really want it;*
> **IF** *it is a good goal;*
> **IF** *you believe you can reach it;*
> **IF** *you work to achieve it;*
> **IF** *you think positively.*

August 15 ————————————————

God has confidence in us. He gives us the power of private judgment. He makes us free moral agents so that we can do what we want to do—even contrary to His will. That is a big God. If God were a little God, He would tell us exactly what to do. But He leaves us free. Still He hopes we are smart enough to do right.

August 16 ————————————————

There's a story about a rusty pickax found in the old Colorado gold country. The handle had long since deteriorated, but the rusted pick remained driven into the ground a hundred years or more. The manner in which it was driven hard into the earth revealed the defeat felt by some frustrated prospector. It seemed to say: "Oh, what's the use? I'm through." The pathetic fact—which this unknown defeated prospector never learned—was that a few yards farther on was a rich vein of gold that later produced millions. If only he had persisted.

August 17 --

A homing pigeon, released in the air, instinctively heads for home. Birds in migration over thousands of miles unerringly return to the same place from which they came. Every rivulet is pulled by the lure of the sea. We come from God; He is our home. Every human life feels the tug of God. The instinct is to return to Him and love Him always.

August 18 --

Hope is like a pointing finger painted on a door that is closed to you. It points, directing you to another door further on that will open to your big opportunity. Look for that other door—that open door.

August 19 --

Some people shrink from going to places that remind them of their departed loved ones; others shrink from doing things that they once did together with others, especially as husband and wife. This is understandable, because it can sharpen the sense of physical loss. The antidote is to remind yourself that the loved person is not only still with you in a spiritual sense but is far more constantly with you than was possible when he or she was alive. When my wife, Ruth, telephoned to tell me my mother had died, she said: "I know you will find this hard to believe right now, Norman, but your mother is going to be with you and nearer to you from now on to a far greater degree than she ever was before. In the past, you have always made plane trips to be with her for a few days or even a few hours. Now she can be with you always." This was true and, once I was able to grasp it, my sense of grief and loss was vastly diminished.

August 20

Storms bring out the eagles; little birds take to cover. Little people try to run from storms and are sometimes smashed by them. But big persons ride storms to better things.

August 21

Many people suffer poor health not because of what they eat but from what is eating them. Emotional ills turn inward, sapping energy, reducing efficiency, causing deterioration in health. And, of course, they siphon off happiness. This situation can be improved by a big daily dose of faith and positive thinking.

August 22

To have friends, be friendly and kindly to everyone. Be happy and outgoing. Get a lot of fun out of everything. Act so that people will have a good opinion of you. Have a spirit-lifting and inspiring personality. Like people. Help those who are having it rough. This is the way to real happiness.

August 23

There is one certain way to decide whether you are old: What is your attitude when you arise in the morning? The person who is young awakens with a strange feeling of excitement, a feeling which he may not be able to explain but which is as if to say, "This is a great day; this is the day on which the wonderful thing will happen." The individual who is old, regardless of age, arises with the spirit unresponsive, not expecting any great thing to happen. This day will be just about like all the rest. The person may hope it will be no worse. Some people retain the spirit of expectation at threescore and ten; some lose it early in life. The measure of one's age is actually how well he retains the romance of youth.

August 24

What a stupendous framework God provides as a setting for our lives! The endless galaxies of innumerable stars; the tempestuous, enormous oceans; the great sighing, surging winds; rolling, reverberating thunder; dashing rain; the drama, mystery, and diversity of the recurring seasons; the thrill of the rising sun and the glory of its going down; the romance of silver moonlight—these are wonders round about us all our lives for us to get thrilled about.

August 25

Be a tough-minded optimist. That is one who does not break apart in the thought processes or attitudes, whatever the stresses. It is one who continues hopefully and cheerfully to expect the good, no matter what the apparent situation. This optimist stays right in there, everlastingly slugging away.

August 26 ----------------------------------

When tension begins rising in my mind, I often find one technique effective. I practice remembered peacefulness, returning mentally to and imaging the most peaceful scenes I have known. I affirm, "The peace of God, which passeth all understanding . . ." (Philippians 4:7).

August 27 ----------------------------------

With faith and patience and sound thinking, you can do many things that "can't be done." Things once thought impossible become possible. As the U.S. Army Corps of Engineers claims: "The difficult we do immediately. The impossible takes a little longer."

August 28 ----------------------------------

When energy runs low and discouragement creeps in, when you have to force yourself to keep going or when some unexpected obstacle throws you and you find it hard to pick yourself up and get going again, it is a time of crisis when the vital factor is simply good old perseverance. Have you got what it takes to stand up and go at it again—and still again? That's the question. Of course you have.

August 29

There is pollution of the mind. If we harbor hate, prejudice, and negativism, we destroy our best thinking potential. We frustrate our highest achievements.

August 30

If you traveled the world over, you would never find another person quite like yourself. Geneticists say if it were possible for one couple to have millions of children, no two would be exactly alike. Because you are different from everyone, there is something which only you can do in this world. The only way you may live a truly creative life, or know the highest happiness, is by being yourself—by developing your own unique potential.

August 31

I do not believe that you can ever be loved unless you truly love other people. Even a dog knows when you love him. I bought an old dog along with my house in the country. I bought him because he came up and put his paw on me and nudged me, looking at me with those beautiful eyes as if to say, "I'm here."

SEPTEMBER

September 1

A person who dislikes himself because of guilt or inferiority feelings will often try to escape painful awareness of this condition by "taking it out on other people." He projects his self-dislike upon others. It is significant that the commandment which begins, "Thou shalt love thy neighbor," concludes with "as thyself" (Leviticus 19:18). If you do not have a normal measure of esteem for yourself, you cannot genuinely like other people. Self-dislike is an enormous obstacle in developing or maintaining good relationships.

September 2

The tough-minded optimist takes a positive attitude toward a fact. He sees it realistically, just as it is, but he sees something more. He views it as a challenge to his intelligence, to his ingenuity and faith. He seeks insight and guidance in dealing with the hard fact. He keeps on thinking. He knows there is an answer and finally he finds it. Perhaps he changes the fact, maybe he just bypasses it, or perhaps he learns to live with it. But in any case his attitude toward the fact has proved more important than the fact itself.

September 3

Prescription: Until condition improves, every day

1. *Take two minutes to think about God.*
2. *Read a psalm.*
3. *Read a chapter from the Gospels.*
4. *Do something kind for someone.*
5. *Get outside yourself by joining some human-betterment effort.*
6. *Go to church every Sunday and get into an atmosphere of faith.*
7. *Become a believer—in God, in life, in yourself.*

September 4

Stronger than willpower is imagination. The word might be pronounced *image-ing*. This means the projection of mental images or pictures of a desired outcome. A basic fact of human nature is the tendency to become like that which we habitually imagine (image) ourselves as being. The deeply held mental image tends to realize itself in fact. If you visualize a goal and hold it firmly in consciousness, the mind has a tendency to complete the image.

September 5

The process of tranquilizing the mind is important in assuring a condition of body, mind, and spirit that will induce perfect rest. Deliberately conceive of the mind as completely quiet, like the surface of a pond on which there is not even a ripple. Picture the mind as motionless and filled with deep quietness. Think silence until an atmosphere of silence seems to surround you. Suggest tranquil ideas to the mind, remembering that your thoughts respond to suggestion. Slowly, deliberately image peace at the center.

September 6

Before this day is out, do something specific and concrete that will demonstrate your determination to change yourself and your life for the better. Pay a debt. Heal a broken relationship. End a quarrel. Offer an apology. Pray for someone. Visit someone who is sick. Restrain yourself from buying something you had planned to buy for yourself and give the money to charity instead. Do whatever you do quietly, without ostentation. And do it, not in hope of reward, but simply because you want to do it, because you prefer to be an inner-directed person.

September 7

On the morning of our thirty-fourth anniversary, Ruth and I went into the church in Syracuse where we were married. How well I remember the day when I first saw her. I was holding a committee meeting following the church service. The door opened and in burst a girl. I had never before seen her but said to myself, *That is the girl for me.* Of course, I had a little job persuading her, but that was the start of a romance that now covers over fifty years. When she and I went into the church on our anniversary, there was no one there. So I said, "Ruth, please go back

91

and burst through that door again.'' She did. Believe me, I would do it all over again! And she says she would, too.

September 8

The average man usually empties his pockets onto his dresser or desk before retiring. Personally, I rather enjoy standing over a wastebasket during this process to see how many things I can throw away: notes, memos, scraps of paper, completed self-directions, even knicknacks which I have picked up. With relief, I deposit all items possible in the wastebasket. It is perhaps more important to empty the mind as one empties pockets. During the day we pick up mental odds and ends: a little worry, a little resentment, a few annoyances, some irritations, perhaps even some guilt reactions. Every night, these should be thrown out for, unless eliminated, they accumulate and subtract from the joy of life.

September 9

A critic is an asset, though perhaps an unpleasant one. Consider criticism objectively and ask whether it is justified. If it is, then try to profit by it, even when it is unfriendly. If it isn't valid, then forget it. Don't criticize in return, just keep on doing your job to the best of your ability. Sure, it hurts, but we are not intended to go through life without some hurt. We are supposed to make strong people of ourselves.

September 10

An old Chinese farmer was walking along the road with a stick across his shoulder. Hanging from the stick was a pot filled with soybean soup. He stumbled and the jar fell off and broke into pieces. The old farmer kept going, unperturbed. A man rushed up and said excitedly, "Don't you know that your jar broke?" "Yes," the old farmer answered, "I know. I heard it fall." "Why didn't you turn around and do something about it?" "It's broken; the soup is gone—what can I do about it?" he asked.

September 11

Here is a good way to end a day and get ready for a great day tomorrow: Do not carry the day into the night. Let it rest while you rest. Before you go to sleep, run over your personal world mentally and thank God for everyone and everything. Count your blessings; name them one by one. Then say to yourself, "God watches over me, over my house, over all my loved ones." Then go to sleep in peace. Let go and let God.

September 12

On the plains, winter storms can take a heavy toll of cattle. The temperature drops below zero. Freezing rain and howling winds whip across the prairie. Snow piles into drifts. In the maelstrom, some cattle, I'm told, turn their backs to the icy blasts and slowly drift downwind, finally coming to a boundary fence barring their way. There they pile against it and many die. But other cattle react differently. They head into the wind, slowly working their way forward against it until they come to a fence. Here they stand, shoulder to shoulder, facing the storm. "We 'most always find them alive and well," said an old cowboy. "That's the greatest lesson I ever learned on the prairie: to attack difficulties head-on and not turn and run."

September 13

Captain Eddie Rickenbacker once gave me an exercise for relaxing: Sit loosely in a chair, making yourself limp. Imagine yourself a burlap bag filled with potatoes. Mentally cut the string, allowing the potatoes to roll out. Be like the bag that remains. Lift your arms one at a time, letting them fall limply. Do the same with your legs and eyelids. Conceive of all your muscles as relaxing. Say, "All tension is subsiding, all stress is leaving me. I am at ease. I am at peace with God, with the world, with myself."

September 14

Think negative thoughts and you thereby activate negative forces and tend to draw back to yourself negative results. Like attracts like. Send out hate and you get back hate. Send out fear and you get back fear. Send out defeat and you draw defeat to yourself. Conversely, send out positive thoughts and positive results will come to you. We defeat ourselves, or gain victories, by the thoughts we think.

September 15

Some persons simply refuse to grow old. I like that eighty-year-old man who told me:

What's wrong with being eighty years old? It isn't how long you've been around; it's what you've done while you've been around. Sure, I've been in the world eighty years. But I don't have an old philosophy. I do not think old thoughts. I happen to own the business I run. But I can still run it all right. When I find some bright young fellow who is as smart as I am, I'll step down. Don't think because I have a game leg that I can't handle the business. You don't run a business with your leg but with your head. And my head is okay. I don't intend ever to get old. I know there will come a time when my obituary will be in the paper, but I will have had the time of my life all my life.

September 16

Rufus Jones, Quaker educator and philosopher, pointed out that the word *individual* implies a being who resists being divided. When you muster yourself on the side of the real you, you come alive, accomplish more, gain a sense of greater worth—and live with joy. The effort it takes to be your own individual really pays off in satisfaction.

September 17

Changing one's thought pattern may be a long and difficult process. But it can be accomplished by the practice of displacing unhealthy thoughts with healthy ones. You can pray out hate, for example. A man told me he had to pray 142 times to get rid of a certain hate but then, like a fever, it broke and he became a well man spiritually and emotionally. Don't knock yourself out disliking or hating or resenting. It isn't easy to shift from that habit to the love habit. But the person who does just that is in for a lot of happiness.

September 18

If your predicament looks hopeless, remember there is no situation so completely dark that something constructive cannot be done about it. When faced with a minus, ask what you can do to make it a plus. Reject hopelessness; substitute faith; use intelligent, persevering effort and you can lift yourself out of hopelessness.

September 19 ━━━━━━━━━━━━━━━━━━━━━━━━

A salesman who from being a loser became a winner, told how he did it:

I went to church one Sunday in a small town where I had to wait over until Monday. In the sermon, the pastor came up with this idea: "You are never going to get the most out of life until you give living all you've got. Don't wait for living to give something to you; you give something to living." This was a new idea to me, exactly what I was not doing. It was as if a door opened in my mind. I had an entire new image of myself and decided I would give living everything I had. So, first thing next morning, I got up earlier than usual, took out the list of people I was going to see that day, and prayed for every one of them. I got to the first store before it opened. I helped the man open up and made my first sale before I would normally even have been up. And I had a wonderful day all day long. It was like magic! All along I had been expecting life to give me something and it hadn't been doing it. Now I was giving something to life and it was giving wonderful things back.

September 20 ━━━━━━━━━━━━━━━━━━━━━━━━

One of professional golf's outstanding players once told me: "One secret of a good shot is 'seeing' the ball going where you want it to go before you hit it.'' And pianists have told me it is possible to practice a number in one's mind without being near a keyboard. You need only visualize the notes with your inner eye and hear them with your inner ear. Whatever your goal, to reach it, fix in your mind a definite and successful outcome. Hold that image and go to work, for you have set in motion a realizable force.

AUTUMN

. . . there is a harmony
In autumn, and a lustre in its sky,
Which through the summer is not heard or seen,
As if it could not be, as if it had not been.

O WROTE PERCY BYSSHE SHELLEY. "HARMONY" and "lustre" are true of autumn. But I also see it as an exciting time of year. Another powerful adjective to associate with autumn is "glorious." "Sensational" and "incredible" go well with it also. For surely woods, aflame with colors that make description difficult, and hills and valleys spread afar like an oriental rug, can hardly be depressing.

Oh, I know where the sadness concept comes from: the dying year, the early twilights, the passing of the fullness of summer, and all that. The last leaf clinging to the moldering wall brings long thoughts tinged with melancholy.

But enough of that. Let's wander, on a late September day or one in crisp October, down a quiet country road in New England or New York or Ohio or Pennsylvania or wherever we can smell autumn. The aroma of burning leaves perfumes the air. Perhaps they contribute something to that "haze on the far horizon, The infinite, tender sky, The ripe rich tint of the cornfields, And the wild geese sailing high." Yes, indeed, as W. H. Carruth says, some of us call it autumn, but others call it God.

Hand in hand, down a winding country road with all this indescribable beauty all about and, at every turn, deep thoughts of home and memories of old days—this is the mystic gift of autumn.

Indian summer it is sometimes called in America, for in bygone years it was said that the haze lingering over the landscape was caused by the fires from the Indian wigwams and tepees. The Indians who peopled the country are long gone, but the old-time autumn haze endures. Could it be that the spirits of the warriors once again come trooping over storied hills and along river valleys famed in song and story in autumn time? Who knows? Many an American, immersed in history and lore, can sense them in the gathering dusk of an October evening. As long as our country endures, the Indian tribes will surely come riding out of the past, down the silvery moon spread of autumn. So it is the mystic time, the romantic interval, the long dream time laced with history still with us, that is called the fall of the year.

And with it comes the music of the falling leaves. Silently they float downward, red, yellow, russet, piling up in windrows until one walks through them ankle deep. Strange about that sound. We became acquainted with it as childhood toddlers. But, at eighty years and beyond, it sounds exactly as it did on long-vanished October days— the rustling of the leaves.

The katydids, who dolefully warned us on September nights that summer was ended and fall had come, are silent now. The nights are still. The big, round harvest moon rides high. The air is cool and crisp. Inside the snug house, the fire burns brightly on the hearth. Apples and walnuts are ready at hand; cider is poured from the jug. It's autumn, it's October, it's America, it's home. There is nothing quite like it in all the world, an American autumn.

September 21

Keep the mouth lines up. Smile and be happy. William James claimed that we are happy because we smile rather than we smile because we are happy. The smile comes first. It is also a fact that happiness in the heart puts a smile on the lips. Cultivate optimism, always looking on the bright side, and you will develop a happy state of life.

September 22

Your mind will give you back exactly what you put into it. If, over a long period of time, you put defeat into your mind, your mind will give you back defeat. But if, over a long period, you put great faith into your mind, your mind will give faith results back.

September 23

Sing at least one song every day. This may not add to the enjoyment of your family or friends, but it will be a wonderful tonic for you. Actually, a hymn is best—a hymn with the morning shower will wash your mind on the inside as soap and water do on the outside.

September 24

Quiet and activity are the opposite sides of creative energy. I doubt that anyone can ever be a creative activist who is not at the same time a creative quietist.

September 25

"Do you ever try talking about God?" I asked a woman whose marriage was not going well. "No," she answered, "my husband talks a great deal about God, but not in the way you mean. When we talk, we argue and quarrel about bills and every unpleasant thing you can think of." I suggested she try returning thanks at the table, for a start. Usually, her husband would sit down and glumly pull up his napkin. Finally, one night, she interrupted softly, "I'm going to return thanks." She did the same the next night, and the next, and the next, until, finally, he said: "Okay, it's my turn. I am going to return thanks!" After that, it was easier to talk about things sanely. They tell me that now their marriage is "in good shape."

September 26

Always start the day with prayer. It is the greatest of all mind conditioners. Even if you do not have the time, pray. It is that important. Always begin the day with the thought of God, His love and care, and with the thought of your responsibility for serving Him. An old friend of mine said it well: "Fill the mind full of God and the whole day will be full of happiness, even if the going gets hard."

September 27

While talking with a physician, I asked what he thought were the physiological advantages of optimism over depression. He told me: Depression in the mind increases the possibility of infection at least tenfold. Optimism actually may help as a force burning out infection. People who maintain a confident attitude have a strange power over sickness. I recommend an attitude of optimism and faith as one of the greatest aids to health.

September 28 --

Here is one week's treatment for tension, uptightness, and stress. Begin it today and continue for the next seven days:

FIRST DAY: *"Peace I leave with you, my peace I give unto you. . . . Let not your heart be troubled, neither let it be afraid"* (John 14:27).

SECOND DAY: *"Thou wilt keep him in perfect peace, whose mind is stayed on thee: because he trusteth in thee"* (Isaiah 26:3).

THIRD DAY: *"My presence shall go with thee, and I will give thee rest"* (Exodus 33:14).

FOURTH DAY: *"Rest in the Lord, and wait patiently for him: fret not thyself . . ."* (Psalms 37:7).

FIFTH DAY: *"Come unto me, all ye that labour and are heavy laden, and I will give you rest"* (Matthew 11:28).

SIXTH DAY: *"Let the peace of God rule in your hearts . . ."* (Colossians 3:15).

SEVENTH DAY: *"He maketh me to lie down in green pastures: he leadeth me beside the still waters. He restoreth my soul"* (Psalms 23:2, 3).

September 29

To combat that "overwhelmed" feeling, use the old military maxim: Concentrate your forces and attack at the point where you may achieve a breakthrough. Don't sit around wringing your hands because so many problems and difficulties beset you. Pick out one, break it down into manageable parts, and go after each part in turn.

September 30

Along in September, up our way, the "line storms" come. High winds of gale force were driving across the ridge on our farm. I heard something groaning and found it was a huge maple tree, 150 years old. But it wasn't groaning; actually it was laughing. It was having the time of its life with that wind. *Maybe it's going to come down*, I thought. "Don't worry," it seemed to say, "I was here before you and I'll be here after you're gone." Oh, trees do go down sometimes, but then what happens? A little shoot comes up and a new tree is started. Human beings are of the same breed. They are absolutely undefeatable when they know they are. But they've got to know it.

OCTOBER

October 1

Fear is the strongest thought pattern, save one. Faith is always stronger than fear. Where faith is, fear cannot live. Faith withers fear. You can crowd fear out by filling your mind with faith. It is an absolute, demonstrable fact that the person who practices faith, real faith in God, rises so high above fear that it can no longer affect that individual.

October 2

Real forgiveness involves no holding back at all. One must go the whole distance in restoring relationships. If one says, "I will forgive you the wrong you have done me, but I can never forget it," that is only qualified forgiveness. To make it real forgiveness, forgetting must be added.

October 3

A businessman told me he was going to fire a certain employee because the man was slow, dull, and sleepy. "Instead of firing him *out* of the business, why not fire him *into* the business?" I asked. "You mean build a fire under him?" he demanded. "No," I said, "build a fire *in* him. Get him excited. Get him motivated." The employer did just that and now he reports of the same employee, "The man is a ball of fire."

October 4 ————————————————————

The Bible gives a tremendous statement which, in the softness of these days, is scarcely ever quoted, at least not often enough. I heard it frequently in the sturdier days of my boyhood: "Quit you like men, be strong" (1 Corinthians 16:13). We simply have to develop sturdiness of will if the tough, hard problems of life are to be handled effectively. Every person has a will. If it is soft, exercise will strengthen it. Think of your will as a "muscle" of the spirit. Like any muscle, if not exercised, it becomes flabby. But, with repeated use, it toughens up, acquiring tone and resiliency.

October 5 ————————————————————

A tornado swept through a southwestern city doing great damage. A mother there, confined to her bed because of infantile paralysis, paralyzed from the waist down, at the height of the tornado became alarmed for her two children in the next room. There was no one to help; the tornado was striking the house with force. Her limbs were assumed to be without power, but concern for the safety of her children was stronger than her limitations. Slowly she got out of bed and painfully made her way into the adjoining room. Taking her babies in her arms, she walked with them out of the house. Love proved more powerful than the paralysis from which she had been told she might never recover. Some people become paralyzed, not in their limbs, but in their thoughts. They accept limitations by saying, "This is all I can do." But that depreciating self-appraisal is not the truth. You are greater than you think you are.

October 6

One of Thomas Jefferson's rules of personal conduct was, "Always take hold of things by the smooth handle." Go at a job or at a difficulty or at a personal-relationship problem by a method that will encounter the least resistance. The less resistance, the faster things move.

October 7

The secret of a successful life is to reduce the error and increase the truth. It is because of the error in us that we make so many mistakes, do so many stupid things, get ourselves into so much trouble, and have things turn out wrong so much of the time. The opposite of error is truth. Jesus Christ said, "I am the way, the truth, and the life" (John 14:6). When we follow Him we follow the truth. The more truth, the fewer errors. It is just that simple.

October 8

Heart is the essence of creative activity. Fire the heart with where you want to go and what you want to be. Get that goal so deeply fixed in your unconscious that you will not take no for an answer. Then your entire personality, your total mentality, will follow where your heart leads. You will go where you want to go, be what you want to be.

October 9

The important fact isn't that we have problems. It is rather our attitude toward problems. There is a small sign in my office that states a big truth: "Attitudes are more important than facts." Of course you cannot ignore a fact, but the attitude of mind with which you approach that fact is all-important.

October 10

Perhaps we have wanted to reach some goal still unattained and to be something which we have not yet accomplished. Let's determine that before this year ends, goals will be reached and dreams come true. Then we will dream new dreams and set higher goals for the years yet to come.

October 11

How do you go about being a happy person? One way is to get into God's rhythm. The heavenly bodies are in rhythm. The internal system of blood and heart and organs are in rhythm. And rhythm is a kind of synonym of harmony, as harmony is one for joy. Therefore, when you are joyful you are in rhythm, and when you are in harmony with God, you are a happy person.

October 12

Five words from the Bible can determine the success of any person or any enterprise: "Seek, and ye shall find" (Matthew 7:7). Seek a need—the world has many. Find a need you can fill and you are on the way to success in life.

October 13 ────────────────────────

A champion golfer says, "What you think while playing golf is probably the most important single part of your game." He stresses the importance of concentration and the practice of visualizing what you want to achieve. The champion confidently projects in his mind the exact direction of flight designed to take the ball where he wants it to go. This principle of imagining also works in determining and reaching goals in life. One must know precisely where he or she wants to go. By firmly visualizing that goal, you force a focus on it and then you can reach it.

October 14 ────────────────────────

It's good to keep our dreams of the future and the thrill of going somewhere ever luring us on. When I was a newspaper reporter, my editor wrote a piece I've kept for years:

> *As a boy of fourteen I stopped Old Bess in the furrow where I was trying to cultivate my father's cornfield. The field was near the railroad track which crossed a trestle. I took off my cap, wiped my brow, and looked up at the fast train of the Baltimore & Ohio Railroad. At every window, as the train sped on, was someone going somewhere. I had never been anywhere, but then and there I made up my mind that someday I would be on my way. I have been on my way ever since, but there are still so many places to go, so many fascinating things to see and do. The train went around the bend. But the dreams of a boy, as the twilight came down, are the dreams I have today. The future beckons with the same mystic allure. It was so in the cornfield; it is so now.*

October 15

A young woman successfully achieved a considerable weight loss—here is what she did: She pictured explicitly the weight she wanted to reach by a certain age. Each time she was tempted, she estimated how long it would take her to eat the gooey desserts, chocolates, or other rich food. Then she thought how happy she would feel after those few minutes had she not eaten it. For the first time she began to experience the thrill of self-mastery. At bedtime, she ran over her temptations mentally and added up all the fattening things she had *not* eaten that day. Eagerly, she looked forward to topping her record the next day. She achieved her weight goal. And she held it, too.

October 16

I have not the slightest doubt concerning the truth and validity of immortality. I believe absolutely and certainly that, when you die, you will meet your loved ones and know them and be reunited with them, never to be separated again. I believe that identity of personality will continue in that greater sphere of life in which there will be no suffering or sorrow as we know them here in the physical sense. I hope there will be struggle, for struggle is good. Certainly there will be ongoing development, for life with no upward effort of the spirit would be incredibly dull. In the teachings of Jesus Christ, death does not refer to the body but rather to the soul: "The soul that sinneth, it shall die" (Ezekiel 18:20). But the soul that is in God will live forever.

October 17

It is never necessary for any individual to live a dull, uninteresting and lackluster life. If one does so, it is because of just letting life become that way. No one needs to live in frustration or allow oneself to become old, worn, and tired. Everyone has the opportunity to open wide the mind and heart, to live a life that is dynamic and exciting. Becoming a positive thinker will help you to have a good day.

October 18

I rode with a man who had the following prayer taped to his instrument panel:

> *Dear Lord, this is Your car. Put Your hands on the steering wheel along with mine and guide me through busy streets and highways. Protect this car from all danger and accident. Give us a safe and pleasant journey. Keep me from getting angry at other drivers. Help me to be polite and observe the rules of the road. Let my driving be a pleasure and not a strain. Amen.*

October 19

One of the greatest blessings in this world is to have good, sound healthy-mindedness. The person who possesses it is most fortunate. Healthy-mindedness is to be a normal, well-balanced, integrated, well-organized human being. It means a mind devoid of inner conflicts and obsessive reactions. The emotional aspect of your nature is under the control of your reason or mind. When you achieve such healthy-mindedness you are free of abnormal fear, free of hate; you are not motivated by resentments; you are free of sulkiness, gloominess, and depressiveness. And such a condition makes for a life that is good every day.

October 20

A good man who had always walked with God approached death. The light was on in his room. Suddenly, a look of surprise crossed the dying man's face. "Turn out the light, the sun is up," he said—and was gone. Apparently it is always light and beautiful over there. But it can be the same here as well when we think it so.

October 21

He lives today no less than long ago. He is alive, not merely as Caesar and Napoleon and Lincoln, for example, are alive—as memories of great men. Jesus is not a memory. He is an actual, contemporary, reachable Person. He is the living Christ, who has the power to enter into people's lives and change and lift them up. Every day the very much alive Lord Jesus is at work among us.

October 22

Here is a prayer to start this day, to help you make it a great day:

Dear Lord, thank You for the night's rest You so graciously gave me. I am grateful for renewed energy and enthusiasm. I accept this new day as a

wonderful opportunity. May I use it minute by min-
ute to do Thy will. Guide me in every problem, every
decision I shall make this day. Help me to treat
everyone kindly and to be fair and just and thoughtful
in everything today. And if I should forget Thee during
this day, O Lord, please do not forget me. Amen.

October 23

A basic fact about every individual is the craving to be
appreciated. One can find happiness by looking for the
best in other people, and that will help bring the best out
of them. And it also helps when we put the best possible
connotation on everyone and everything. Faith in people
and a positive attitude can release these tremendous re-
sources that are resident in everyone.

October 24

I continually advocate that you be a true optimist, rugged
mentally, a real believer. No doubt-thinking person can be
an optimist, for an optimist is a person who believes in
good outcomes even when he can't yet see them. That is
also the Bible's definition of *faith* as "the substance of
things hoped for, the evidence of things not seen." So the
real believer is a person who believes in better things when
there is yet no evidence to confirm his expectation. He is
one who believes in his own future even when he cannot
see much possibility in it.

October 25

Get worked up about your job and you will work your job
up. Get fired up about it and you will put fire into it. Any

human occupation has excitement in it if you have excitement in you. And how do you find this excitement? A famous French writer answered with these words: "Faith is an excitement and an enthusiasm: it is a condition of intellectual magnificence to which we must cling as a treasure."

October 26 ————————————————————

Here are five simple and workable rules for overcoming inadequacy attitudes and for learning to believe in yourself:

1. *Formulate and stamp indelibly on your mind a mental picture of yourself as succeeding. Hold this picture tenaciously. Never permit it to fade. Your mind will seek to develop this picture as fact. Never think of yourself as failing; never doubt the reality of the mental image.*

2. *Whenever a negative thought concerning your ability comes to mind, deliberately voice a positive thought to cancel it out.*

3. *Do not build obstacles in your imagination. Depreciate every so-called obstacle. Minimize them. Difficulties must be studied and efficiently dealt with, but they must be seen only for what they are. They must not be inflated by fear thoughts.*

4. *Do not be awestruck by other people or try to copy them. Nobody can be you as efficiently as you can.*

5. *Ten times a day repeat these words: "If God be for me, who can be against me?" (see Romans 8:31).*

October 27 ━━━━━━━━━━━━━━━

Experience bears out the thesis that things go wrong because we are wrong. If we resolutely seek to understand where we're wrong and make changes, we are on our way to better things. "Most of the shadows of this life," said Ralph Waldo Emerson, "are caused by standing in our own sunshine." When we get busy changing attitudes that have been casting shadows and making things go wrong, then things start going right. A changed person changes situations and conditions.

October 28 ━━━━━━━━━━━━━━━

We are continuously building up or breaking down the self. Through the years, every thought, every emotion, every experience contributes to the quality of self. No matter how old or how set we become, self is in the making. Everything contributes to its greatness or littleness, its stagnation or growth. What will *your* contribution be today?

October 29 ━━━━━━━━━━━━━━━

When you attain a sense of undefeatableness, you will always be high-spirited and confident. Spirit is taken out of you when you allow yourself to be overwhelmed, nonplussed, and stymied by circumstances and conditions. An important secret of success is to get yourself firmly based in spiritual understanding, in faith and positive thinking. Then nothing, no matter what, can defeat you. You will have attained indomitability.

October 30

Basic in living creatively is to accept pain and difficulty as a challenge. God, who made this universe, gives us difficulties for our own best interest. He wants to make something of us and people do not grow strong in soft and fortuitous circumstances. Struggle toughens personality.

October 31

Ever practice remembered peacefulness? I think of a favorite spot in Switzerland, remembering how, at evening time, the snows on the mountains change coloring from brilliant gold to mystic purple and then fade into the dark. I think of a night on the China Sea when mists veiling the face of the moon were blown aside by a gentle breeze to allow long, silvery shafts of moonlight to fall on limpid waters. I think of a night at Srinagar in the Vale of Kashmir, where the sound of singing boatmen came across the lake on the surface of which water lilies floated. Once in my doctor's office, my pulse and blood pressure readings were taken. "Well!" he said, "that's fine. You have learned to live calmly." I told him the technique of remembered beauty to help promote tranquillity. He nodded. "Good, that helps in keeping healthy."

NOVEMBER

November 1

You and I, ten years from now, will be mostly what we think during that period. You can think yourself to failure and unhappiness, or you can think your way to success and real happiness. Better give your thoughts a good overhauling once in a while. Think good days today and you'll have them tomorrow as well.

November 2

An uptight man once said to me, speaking of New York, "The very air of this city is filled with tension." "Not so," I said. "If you were to take a sampling of this air to a laboratory for analysis, you wouldn't find a trace of tension in the air. You see, tension is in the minds of people who breathe the air."

November 3

One man's rules for making a success in life are:

1. *Practice the affirmation of God's presence daily.*
2. *Pray for those with whom you work and deal.*

3. *Image success not only for yourself but also for your competitors.*
4. *Try to live by faith.*

November 4

George Cullum, Sr., Dallas construction executive, had a formula for himself and his men. He used to say: "When the job gets tough, get as tough as the job. When the rock gets hard, get as hard as the rock." Life can be tough, really tough. But God built something in human nature that is tougher still. Draw on it.

November 5

Take minute vacations during the day. Sit back in your office chair. Close your eyes and, in memory, go away to some place that means a lot to you, such as where you like to fish or play golf, or swim. Letting the mind go away, if only for a moment, tones up the body with an infusion of fresh energy.

November 6

A successful businessman told me what had turned the tide for him when he was doing poorly. It was a picture of a boat stuck in the sand, the tide out. The title of that picture was *The Tide Always Comes Back*. Don't ever accept defeat. Never even think, *I can't*. Instead, say to yourself, "The tide always comes back." It will, if you will it so.

November 7

As a boy I had an enormous inferiority complex and, believe me, it was no fun. I used to go around thinking negatively: "I don't amount to anything. I have few brains and no ability." I became aware, after a while, that others were agreeing with me. They always will— for, unconsciously, people will take you at your own self-appraisal.

November 8

The world offers so much fun and pleasure. It is pathetic how little of it many people find. Thousands live in what might be called "pleasure poverty" despite the available wealth of fun opportunities. They keep their noses to the grindstone and develop a sad crop of neuroses and tensions. Work is good but, when it's mixed with fun, it's a lot better. Don't be a fun pauper! Revel in the delights a good God has put into the world!

November 9

How to relax? Repeat slowly and quietly, bringing out the melody in each, a series of words which express quietness and peace, as, for example, tranquillity (say it very deliberately and in a tranquil manner), serenity, quietness, imperturbability. Say the following, which has an amazing power to quiet the mind and relax the body: "Thou wilt keep him in perfect peace, whose mind is stayed on thee" (Isaiah 26:3). Repeat this several times during the day and you will find relaxation.

November 10

A salesman was having trouble making sales, always afraid, forever whistling in the dark. An older salesman gave him a three-sentence prayer. The results were miraculous and his percentage of sales rose steadily. This is the prayer he used: "I believe I am always divinely guided. I believe I will be led always to take the right turn of the road. I believe that God will always make a way where there is no way."

November 11

An important question for anyone is: What am I doing to my own self? Am I making myself big to equate with the power potential in me? Or am I accepting smallness as all I am capable of? To think yourself smaller than you are is a violation of your real nature. Think big.

November 12

Rural wisdom: On the platform of a small-town railroad station years ago, two men and a dog watched the express train streak past. The dog went racing after it—and was still chasing and barking at it when the last car vanished in the distance. "Crazy fool dog! Does he think he can catch the Empire State Express?" snorted the stationmaster. After a reflective silence, his friend observed, "And what would he do with it if he did?"

November 13

There are rules to follow if you wish to get along with others:

1. *Know the names of all with whom you associate and speak to them by name.*
2. *Be quick with praise.*
3. *Always be constructive if it is necessary to criticize.*
4. *Keep your temper under control.*
5. *Always be ready to lend a helping hand.*
6. *Readily admit your own mistakes and never hesitate to say, "I'm sorry."*
7. *Take a real interest in the organization which employs you.*
8. *Seek no acclaim for achievement but always give someone else the credit due him or her.*
9. *Assume that other people like you.*
10. *Try to like and esteem other people as you would have them like and esteem you.*

November 14

An old Oriental maxim says, "What you think upon grows." You tend to become what you think of yourself as being. Raise your appraisal of yourself. Affirm that you have greater possibilities than have ever yet appeared. Don't self-limit yourself, even in your private thoughts. Always see yourself as greater than you have ever been.

November 15

Want to give up smoking or, for that matter, anything else? The desire to smoke is basically one of thought, plus a nervous impulse to do something with the hands. Also involved is the infantile tendency to put something in the mouth. To quit, decide you really want to quit. Intense desire is always basic in achieving or quitting. Then, decide you are really going to quit. Finally, picture yourself as being released from the habit. Hold that picture firmly and tenaciously until your subconscious mind accepts it. Do not try to taper off—stop entirely. Ask God to help you and believe that He will. The desire is primarily in your mind—think victory thoughts and images. To cure the nervous movement of the hands, practice control of muscle tension. Believe you can—and you can.

November 16

Repeat these four statements when tense and uptight:

> *From Confucius: "The way of a superior man is threefold: virtuous, therefore free from anxiety; wise, therefore free from perplexity; bold, therefore free from fear."*

> *From Robert Louis Stevenson: "Sit loosely in the saddle of life."*

> *From Saint Theresa, a sixteenth-century mystic: "Let nothing disturb you; let nothing frighten you. Everything passes except God; God alone is sufficient."*

> *From Isaiah: ". . . in quietness and in confidence shall be your strength" (Isaiah 30:15).*

November 17

The word *resentment* means to re-feel—to feel again. Someone wrongs or wounds you; in resenting it, you re-feel the injury. And you re-hurt yourself. The Hebrew Talmud says that a person who bears a grudge is "like one who, having cut one hand while handling a knife, avenges himself by stabbing the other hand." The best way to avoid this self-inflicted suffering is to apply "spiritual iodine" the moment anybody hurts you. Get your resentment healed at once, before it starts to fester.

November 18

The more we apply mental power against seemingly hopeless difficulties and follow the flashes of insight which come from real thinking, the surer our accomplishment. Thinking gives one the daring to do the unusual when a situation calls for it: a readiness to shift thinking quickly when problems turn out differently than anticipated.

November 19

Problems are a normal and essential part of all of life. Strength develops from standing up to them, thinking them through, and mastering them. By approaching problems in a positive frame of mind, you can always derive good from them, no matter how difficult they may be.

November 20

No matter how dark things become, someone is always with you—and that someone is God. He helps by giving you peace and a positive mental attitude. With these, you can start real creative thinking and, as a result, will be able to take a hopeful and not a negative view. Such dynamic thinking will start things coming your way and presently you will find yourself on top of trouble.

November 21

Thanksgiving is a grateful recognition of past benefits and the activator of blessings yet to come. Thankfulness stimulates a continuous flow of blessings. If, in your life, there is a paucity of blessings, it may be that your practice of thankfulness has grown weak and inactive. The attitude of gratitude is important in achieving wholeness in life. Only by enumerating the many blessings bestowed upon us can we fully appreciate the generous bounty of God.

November 22

Really, there is one thing that you must never do. You must never, as long as you live, stop believing in yourself! You were made by God, the Creator, and He never made anything badly. When He made you, He made you good, very good. And, therefore, you have the right to hold a high opinion of yourself. A good, healthy self-respect is normal and right. So have a great day today and a great life always.

November 23

Fear lurks among shadows and thrives in darkness. A spiritually darkened mind is a breeding ground for terrifying fears. But, when the mind is filled with the Lord's presence, it is automatically also filled with light. Intelligent thinking follows and fears are driven off. "The Lord is my light . . . whom shall I fear?" (Psalms 27:1).

November 24

To have mental health and live successfully, every person must move away from past failures and mistakes and go forward without letting them weigh upon the mind. Never dwell upon the "ifs" but rather upon the "hows." Forgetting is absolutely necessary to a successful future. Every night, when you lie down to sleep, practice dropping all failures and mistakes into the past. They are over, finished. Look confidently to the future. Go to sleep in peace. God gives you new opportunities every morning.

November 25

Here is a prayer to help you to forgive: Lord, You tell us to forgive our enemies. This I want to do—or do I, really? But Lord, I do not know how to forgive—or is it that I just haven't the moral strength to do so?

Deliver me from nursing a grudge. Help me to want to forgive.

Fill my mind with magnanimous thoughts. Make me bigger than I've been acting. Let me know the joy of forgiveness and reconciliation. The Bible says, "For if ye forgive men their trespasses, your heavenly Father will also forgive you" (Matthew 6:14). So please take my enemy off my hands. And I thank You that I find it in my heart to say, "Be good to him or her." Amen.

November 26

Many factors determine the way we go and how we go and where we arrive in life. But one thing is for sure: If you forget those things which are behind, as the Bible teaches, and reach forward toward those things which are ahead, pressing "toward the mark for the prize of the high calling of God in Christ Jesus" (Philippians 3:14), you have a future that will be full of achievement and joy.

November 27

The Bible tells us that the sins of the fathers are passed on to succeeding generations. The virtues of the fathers can be passed along, too. If a father is an honest and upright man, and if he establishes any sort of adequate relationship with his sons and daughters, it is going to be very hard for those children to get off the track, or getting off, not to get back on. The desire to emulate and imitate is too strong.

November 28

Prayer of a distracted parent: Dear Lord, I love my children but they are driving me to distraction. I have lost my self-control. I need help. I realize, dear Lord, that I can never direct them in their young lives if I am disorganized. Help me not to be angry and not to shout at them. Give me a sense of humor. Help me to know that their restless energy is a sign of vitality and part of their development. Don't let me be tired and upset but rather enter joyfully into my relationship with them.

Thank You for my children, Lord, but, don't let them get me down. Amen.

November 29

My brother, Bob, and I used to fight each other occasionally, but if any other boy attacked either of us, he had both of us to contend with. We have been inseparable all our lives; our fighting ended a long time ago. Our love is lifelong—and even beyond. The love of our brothers and sisters is a gift for which we should be grateful.

November 30 ———————————————

In one sense, the big issue of our personal life is the competition between error and truth. When error is in the saddle and rides us, we do dumb things and spend a lot of time regretting them. When truth is in control, we stay on the beam and handle life's problems masterfully.

DECEMBER

December 1

Two words—*deny yourself*—are important to self-control. They may relate to success or to failure. Refuse the candy, skip second helpings, don't buy the dress, don't goof off—where will *you* start to say no to yourself? Don't consider it a decision *against* some form of fun but a decision *for* a desired goal in your life. This makes it a positive, not a negative step. This isn't taking the joy out of life. Actually it's putting the joy into life. The more we give up to concentrate on an important goal, the stronger we become. Self-denial in the present, to gain greater benefits in the future, is the hallmark of a rational human being.

December 2

My wife, Ruth, was at a church dinner out west and was seated across from a farmer. His hands and windblown look showed how he had toiled. She asked, "How are the crops this year?" "Ma'am," he replied, "we had a long drought, then came the grasshoppers. I lost ninety percent of my crop. But my brother lost all of his." Appalled,

131

Ruth asked, "But what did your brother do?" Quietly, he answered, "We just aimed to forget it." Next year offers a new beginning.

December 3

On an airplane in the Far East, in typhoon season, I asked the pilot how he handled those strong winds. "Oh," he replied, "I turn typhoons into tailwinds!" In life there are many troubles, some seemingly as big as typhoons. With faith in God and by using the mind He gave you, you can learn the laws that govern trouble. Then you can turn difficulty into opportunity and make it speed you on your way with a strong tailwind to achievement.

December 4

How do you draw on a higher power? Practice living with God. Live with Him every day. Be with Jesus Christ. Talk to Him. Have conversation with Him as a friend. Pray to Him. Think about Him. Do not do anything, however seemingly small or insignificant, without bringing Him into it. The more you do this, the more you will identify with divine forces, and the power flow from them to you will increase.

December 5

By dwelling too much upon mistakes you can keep yourself in an error groove. Mistakes can be teachers—but they can also be leeches, clinging to your thinking, conditioning you to make the same mistakes again. It is all too easy to let yesterday's mistakes ruin today. Train your mind to learn from your successes.

December 6

At any point in our lives each of us is standing on a kind of moral ladder. There are rungs above us and rungs below. We can climb up or we can step down. Or we can simply stand still, which is the easiest thing to do, because it requires no effort and involves no risk. What we really have to do if we are interested in self-development is make up our minds to move up a rung and then another and another on the moral ladder.

December 7

One man checks on the rightness or wrongness of a proposed action this way: He visualizes his role reported in big black headlines in tomorrow's newspaper. If something in him winces at the thought, he tells himself he had better censor that action.

December 8

Never laugh off anyone who has an evangelical zeal for or against anything. A single individual with strong and zealous determination can stimulate amazing forces which may become dominant, even when a vast majority disagrees. A fat, sleepy majority can be pushed around by a few persons aflame with positive conviction or negative destructiveness. Both are powerful motivators. Fortunately, positive convictions are more powerful than negative ones.

December 9

When trouble strikes, what you want is not only comfort and sympathy. You want strength to stand up to it and meet it. You can have both. Remind yourself that God is with you, that He will never fail you, that you can count upon Him. Say these words: "God is with me, helping me" and "God is our refuge and strength, a very present help in trouble." This will give you a sense of comfort. New hope will flood your mind. Emotional reaction will give way to rational thinking. New ideas will come. A new sense of strength will be yours. Result—you will rise above your trouble.

December 10

A pilot told me that some of the big jet airplanes have a series of blades extending down the wings which cause air to swirl toward the rear of the plane. This provides the necessary turbulence for directional accuracy in flight. If the air is too smooth, some roughness has to be added to improve flight conditions. Perhaps suffering and hardship serve the same purpose for a human being. Maybe we need "turbulence" to help us develop a sense of direction so that we may ultimately reach the destination intended for us in life.

December 11

Arve Hatcher tells how, after a heavy blizzard, his car was stuck in a snow pile, and his efforts to get it moving only dug its wheels in deeper and deeper. Down the street came a muscular teenager carrying a shovel. When he saw the problem he promptly got to work and set the car free. "Many thanks," Hatcher said gratefully, and reached to hand him some folded bills. "No way," the teenager said with a smile. "I belong to the DUO Club." "Never heard of it," Hatcher replied. "Sure you have," the boy grinned.

"It's the do-unto-others-as-you-would-have-them-do-unto-you club." And with a wave of his hand and another big smile, he was on his way.

December 12

To have courage, think courage. We become what we think. As you think courage, courage will fill your thoughts and displace fear. The more courageous your thinking, the greater the courage you will have. Act courageously. Practice the "as if" principle. Act as if you are courageous and you will become as you think and act. A person should pray for courage as he prays for his daily bread. And your prayer for courage will enable you to think and act with courage.

December 13

Set apart a regular time to deliberately still your thoughts and emotions so that you may commune with your deeper self. When the mind is agitated by the noise, hurry, and confusion of modern life, you cannot truly consult the creative depths within yourself where lie answers to your perplexing problems. Remember Thomas Carlyle's words: "Silence is the element in which great things fashion themselves together."

December 14

Dare to be what you ought to be; dare to be what you dream to be; dare to be the finest you can be. The more you dare, the surer you will be of gaining just what you dare. But if you go at things timorously, telling yourself,

"I'm afraid I'll never make it" or "I just know I can't do it" or "I haven't got what it takes," then you will get a result in kind. Dream great dreams; dare great dreams. Have great hopes; dare great hopes. Have great expectations, dare great expectations. ". . . the Lord is the strength of my life . . . in this will I be confident" (Psalms 27:1, 3).

December 15

An enemy of worry is reason. Hit your anxiety hard with reason. Worry is an emotion; reason is a sound mental process. No emotion can stand long against cool, factual, reasoned analysis. Spread your worry out and apply reason to it. Take it apart and see how its constituent elements fade in the presence of reason.

December 16

Christianity is not only a philosophy; it not only a theology. It is also a science. A science is any body of truth that is based on demonstrable formulas. Jesus gives us such formulas. If you love, you will get loving results; if you hate, you will get hateful results. He tells us that, if we live a good life, we will experience inner joy. Christianity works for all who try it.

December 17

Our taxi made about two blocks in fifteen minutes that Christmas season. "This traffic is terrible," my companion growled. "It draws off what little Christmas spirit I've got." My other companion was more philosophical. "It sure is something," he mused, "really something. Just think of it. A baby born more than nineteen hundred years ago, over five thousand miles away, causes a traffic jam on Fifth Avenue. Yep, that sure is something!''

December 18

I often think of my grandmother, how she would talk with God and about God, as simply as with her next-door neighbor. She talked to me when I was a lad, about God as a kindly Father, about Christ as the Head of the house. She had a framed placard hung up which read, "Christ is the head of this house, the Unseen Listener to every conversation. . . ." Christ was around about at all times. He was very near because Grandma and Grandpa practiced religious conversations. In those days they shared their spiritual experiences and talked about the deep things of life. Sharing God brings you closer to Him.

December 19

Everyone has both a best and a worst side. A poet once said, "There is an unseen battlefield in every human breast where two opposing forces meet and where they seldom rest." For every human being the great issue is which of the two shall triumph and prevail in him, the worst or the best? You must pray for the best.

December 20

"This is the refreshing . . ." said the prophet Isaiah (28:12). These few words remind us of a spring of cool water. They have a renewing quality. The frequent use of this text has an invigorating effect. After a busy day or in the midst of tiring details, as in Christmas activities, stop and say these words over to yourself and note how they dissipate weariness and refresh the body, mind, and spirit. Say them slowly, emphasizing their soft and quiet melody. At the same time, conceive of peace, rest, and renewal as coming to you. They will.

WINTER

WINTER! SOME DO NOT LIKE IT MUCH, BUT ENDURE IT. Others go away from it to warmer climates and sojourn among palm trees and on sandy beaches warmed by a golden sun. Followers of perennial summer and devotees of higher temperatures, they have long since lost acquaintance with winter's rugged delights.

But some of us are devoted lovers of the four seasons. Having lived among them for so long, the changing of the seasons is our inherited life-style. And while, now and then, we grumble at the ice and snow, we really don't mind winter all that much and, believe it or not, we like it most of the time.

A summer night in June or July can be of entrancing beauty and charm, but the same may be said of many a winter evening in December or January. It is a time of snow crunching underfoot, the night clear and cold, brilliant stars in the sky, moonlight so bright it rivals noonday. The glorious colors of warmer areas are beautiful beyond the ability to describe them, especially when one tries to convey the exotic fragrances of tropical or semitropical flowers. But then, black and white can be beautiful, too, either separately or in combination.

Only recently, returning from a winter afternoon's walk on our farm on Quaker Hill, Ruth and I simultaneously stopped, arrested by the beauty of the scene before us. Our house atop a hill stood etched in white against a blue sky, its stately Corinthian columns gleaming in the early setting of the sun in the west. Snow lay deep upon the ground, festooned on bushes and trees. The long white fences ran off into the distance, lined by gigantic maples, stark and black against the white-clad hills. Long shafts of golden sunlight lay across the snow-covered lawns as the winter evening came down cold and stern. This beauty was of black and white to which gold was added. Ruth enthusiastically agreed when I exclaimed, "In its own glorious way, this just has to be as beautiful as that lovely southland."

"Yes," she replied, "but isn't all of God's great world beautiful, north or south or wherever?"

Winter silences have their meaningful appeal to the reflective mind. Gliding cross-country on skis into a lonely grove of trees, then standing still and quiet until the palpable silence makes itself felt is, in a deep sense, to be at one with the essence of life. I have been alone in the same grove of trees in midsummer, but nature is not so silent then—for aliveness is all around. In winter, nature's utter and incredible stillness steals upon one, though at either time the healing of her gentle touch is felt.

But whether it is the tentative change of nature's springtime, or the fullness of her summer, or the flaming glory of autumn, or finally, the disciplinary cold of winter, the good God made them all for us.

December 21 ━━━━━━━━━━━━━━━━━━━━━━

Perhaps courage is a basic life quality which God gives us. It builds up the spirit in crises. Moments may come when courage alone stands between us and disaster. In the long pull, across the years, there will be times when we need dogged courage to keep us going when the going is hard. And what is the source of such rugged courage? It is surely that sense of God's presence when we hear Him say, "I am with you always."

December 22 ━━━━━━━━━━━━━━━━━━━━━━

Our children are the citizens of the future who must be taught not to lie and cheat but to be honest people like the sturdy and decent forefathers who forged our great country. Dishonest living is a blow at the United States itself, for a free land can survive only through men and women of integrity. Tell them that the Child of Bethlehem came to make people good.

December 23 ━━━━━━━━━━━━━━━━━━━━━━

What greater happiness can come to a family than the arrival of a baby! Surely it is a sign that God has blessed that marriage and that home. A baby is God's masterpiece—a wonderful creation of His infinite mind. The arrival of baby Jesus brought a great and exciting happiness into the world.

December 24 ━━━━━━━━━━━━━━━━━━━━━━

The poet James Russell Lowell wrote in "A Christmas Carol":

And they who do their souls no wrong,
But keep at eve the faith of morn,
Shall daily hear the angel-song,
"Today the Prince of Peace is born!"

There's a lifelong glory to the Christmas season, from wide-eyed childhood to old age. It's an inexpressible glory. Keep it that way always.

December 25

The Christmas story is ushered in with a song, ". . . and on earth peace, good will toward men" (Luke 2:14). Everyone was joyful, for something wonderful had happened. A great Teacher had come to earth to tell the simple secret of peace and joy. And what a secret it is. When we have peace in our hearts, we also have love in our hearts and good will toward all men. Who but our Lord could have thought of such a simple way to happiness? And our Saviour, whose birth we celebrate this Christmas day, saves us from our sins and receives us to eternal life. No wonder we happily say to each other today, "Merry Christmas!"

December 26

We are much disturbed by antagonisms held by other people toward us but usually little concerned by the unfriendly feelings we have for them. We think the other man ought to change, but give little consideration to the possibility that we ourselves ought to change. To get changed spiritually ourselves—that is the real solution. The spirit of Christmas can help us to do that.

December 27

A physician says that 70 percent of his patients reveal resentment in their case histories. "Ill will and grudges help to make people sick. Forgiveness," he says, "will do more toward getting them well than many pills." So it is healthy to forgive, to say nothing of its being the right way to live. Develop the habit of looking for people's good points. Everybody has them. This thought may help you get ready for great days in the upcoming new year.

December 28

Marcus Aurelius, the Roman emperor, said: "Life is what our thoughts make it." Saint Paul said substantially the same thing: ". . . be ye transformed by the renewing of your mind . . ." (Romans 12:2). This is the great secret that Christianity has given people across the centuries, changing them from desultory to vital, from dead to alive, from weak to strong, from dull to alert. "I live; yet not I, but Christ liveth in me" (Galatians 2:20).

December 29

As the old year runs out, one of the most important skills you can cultivate is the ability to forget. If you really want to move away from failures and unpleasant experiences, you've got to be able to say, "Okay, I've had it—now I'll forget it." Then do just that. ". . . forgetting those things which are behind, and reaching forth . . . I press toward the mark . . ." (Philippians 3:13, 14).

December 30

To start your new year right, I suggest finding a deeper spiritual life. Something happens deep within you and thereafter you are filled with joy and warmth and beauty. This may happen quickly and dramatically. It could happen today. On the other hand, it may be a developing experience, unfolding as a rose, beginning with a bud and ending with full flowering. But, however it happens, this is the greatest experience possible to a human being.

December 31

Here is a New Year's Eve thought to ensure a great day every day beginning now. Saint Paul says, ". . . walk in newness of life" (Romans 6:4). What does that mean? It simply means to get rid of all these old barnacles that have encrusted you for so long: resentments, dishonesties, rationalizations, fears, weaknesses, and so on. These must all go, so that you may "walk in newness of life." When you're new, you *feel* like walking, head up, standing tall, for you have fresh new power. That God may reactivate your life so that you may "walk in newness of life," why not just be done with some things. Get so tired of the old, so fed up with it, that you are done with it. If you've been full of fear, be done with being full of fear. If you've been full of error and defeat, be done with it. Say, "By God's grace, I'm done with it," and take charge of yourself like never before. And, for certain, it will be a Happy New Year for you.

About the Author

NORMAN VINCENT PEALE remains one of the most widely read inspirational writers of all time. He is coeditor and copublisher (with his wife of over sixty years, Ruth) of *Guideposts* magazine and is Senior Minister of the Collegiate Reformed Protestant Dutch Church of the City of New York. The recipient of many awards throughout his long and illustrious career, including the Presidential Medal of Freedom, he continues to write, travel, and lecture extensively.

Insight and Inspiration...

from

NORMAN VINCENT PEALE